Study Guide

for

Burger's

Personality

Sixth Edition

Thomas L. Wilson
Bellarmine University

THOMSON
WADSWORTH

Australia • Canada • Mexico • Singapore • Spain • United Kingdom • United States

Printed in Canada
1 2 3 4 5 6 7 07 06 05 04 03

Printer: Webcom

ISBN: 0-534-52797-3

Cover image: Trevor Wood/Getty Images

Wadsworth/Thomson Learning
10 Davis Drive
Belmont, CA 94002-3098
USA

Asia
Thomson Learning
5 Shenton Way #01-01
UIC Building
Singapore 068808

Australia/New Zealand
Thomson Learning
102 Dodds Street
Southbank, Victoria 3006
Australia

Canada
Nelson
1120 Birchmount Road
Toronto, Ontario M1K 5G4
Canada

Europe/Middle East/South Africa
Thomson Learning
High Holborn House
50/51 Bedford Row
London WC1R 4LR
United Kingdom

Latin America
Thomson Learning
Seneca, 53
Colonia Polanco
11560 Mexico D.F.
Mexico

Spain/Portugal
Paraninfo
Calle/Magallanes, 25
28015 Madrid, Spain

For all students who
want to learn and learn well

Contents

Preface

To the Student

This study guide has been designed to help you succeed in your personality psychology course. Performing the activities provided in these pages will aid you in understanding the textbook, but this study guide does not replace the textbook material. With proper regular use of the study guide you will master the most important facts, concepts, and key issues presented in the text. You will grow in your knowledge of the fundamental approaches to personality and their application, of personality assessment and research. Finally, this study guide will help you be prepared for course examinations and provide you with confidence in your knowledge.

Each chapter of the study guide corresponds to a chapter in the textbook. There are several sections in each chapter that provide different learning activities to help you move beyond mere passive reading to take command of the textbook topics. These sections include the opening outline, Learning Objectives, Important Concepts, Programmed Review, Multiple Choice Questions, Integrative Questions, and Evaluative Questions. Performing these learning activities will increase your understanding on several levels, some at the level of facts and applications and some at the levels of analysis, integration, and critical evaluation. Plan your study time to include these learning activities. They are based on cognitive learning strategies supported by research and they lead to better comprehension and retention of knowledge.

The following is a description of study strategies that make use of the learning activities in each chapter of this study guide with instructions on how to perform each one effectively. Of course, only you can determine for yourself how to best use this study guide, how much time and effort you will put into your study efforts, and what sections work best for you. We urge you to give each activity a try before passing judgment on its effectiveness as a learning strategy. Following these guidelines, you will be able to practice and develop your learning skill.

A Strategy for Learning

Organized around learning objectives, the activities in this study guide have been designed to exercise and elaborate your knowledge in memory. A fundamental property of the human mind is that information more deeply processed is more accurately and reliably retained in memory. It is strongly suggested that you begin every textbook chapter with a brief review of the *structure* of the chapter given in the opening outline. An understanding of the organization of material to be learned is essential to the task.

Then, before opening the textbook to begin reading, *carefully read* the Learning Objectives and pause to consider what to expect. Then read the textbook chapter. The remainder of the study guide activities are recommended after you have read the chapter to achieve better processing and retention of the textbook material.

Each chapter of this study guide begins with an opening outline that reveals the structure of chapter topics. Try to get an overall sense of the organization of the textbook material as a first step toward forming relationships among topics and organizing your knowledge. Research has shown that having the topical organization in mind prior to study encourages active rather than passive text reading and improves comprehension.

Learning Objectives

Following the opening outline you will find a list of expectations titled "Learning Objectives." At first glance the list may appear long and tedious because of its detail and resemblance to essay questions. Work over these objectives in small steps; do not try to master the entire list in one long study session. The Learning Objectives make up a comprehensive list of the *abilities* you should acquire in your mastery of the textbook material. When you can demonstrate to yourself that you have acquired these abilities by actually being able to do them, then you can be completely confident in your knowledge from the textbook.

The Learning Objectives should be carefully reviewed *before* reading each textbook chapter or chapter section. You are not expected to have these abilities yet; just read about them. Once the Learning Objectives are firmly in mind, the material you read in the textbook will jump out at you and engage you in active and purposeful reading. Some students find it helpful to create their own short essay-type test to monitor their understanding as they read and study the textbook. Most successful students have developed the ability to self-monitor as they study; the learning objectives can serve this function. After studying some textbook material, go back to the Learning Objectives and use them as short essay questions. Write your answers as best you can. If you don't have the answer to a question, then go back to the textbook for more study. As a diagnostic tool, answering the Learning Objectives will provide you with useful feedback about the abilities that need more of your attention and further study.

Important Concepts

A list of the most important concepts from each chapter (usually highlighted in bold or italics in the text) is provided for easy study of the most basic form of knowledge: facts and concepts. It is essential to do more than just memorize facts and definitions. Try to *relate* concepts to one another as you study. Ask yourself how each concept in the textbook relates to other concepts or the section heading in which it is found. Also, it helps to be able to *generate* an example of your own of each term and concept in the text. In contrast to rote memorization, when students give their own examples of new ideas and concepts the knowledge is more deeply processed in memory and, as a result, one's retention and application of textbook material is greatly enhanced. Simply write out your own example for each concept in the list. For each important concept listed, the textbook page number is given where you can find the concept discussed and/or defined.

Some students may find it helpful to create flash cards of these concepts and their definitions, or flash cards of the concepts and examples, to take with them in their daily activities. Repetition is a fundamental strategy that the mind uses to improve memory, so repetitive learning through flash cards can be beneficial if you use them effectively! Avoid including too much information on any given card. Although it may seem better to have a lot of information memorized from flash cards, too much information defeats the purpose of rote rehearsal that flash cards provide. Also, avoid learning from more than 20 flash cards at a time. Again, too much at one time can interfere with memory rather than improve it. It is better to take 5 or 6 cards with you each day to class or work to review during free time or study time before doing more.

InfoTrac. At the end of the list of Important Concepts you will find some search terms for which you can use the InfoTrac Online Library, a fully searchable online university library with access to full articles from thousands of periodicals. With your personal passcode, you can enter a word or words in the "Subject Guide" from your computer and the search procedure will take you to a reference list of articles related to that topic. From there you can gain access to the full text of these articles. The online library is easy to use and "hooks you up" to in-depth information on topics from the text. See the *InfoTrac Flowchart* presented in the last pages of this study guide for further details on what to do.

Programmed Review

Students and educators alike often mistake this portion of each chapter as fill-in-the-blank questions. While these require you to fill in blanks, the Programmed Review can be much more than simply filling in, if you use it as suggested here. It is understood that most students would rather scrub their bathtub or apartment with a wire brush than do a series of fill-in questions. As you will discover, the Programmed Review learning activity is designed to help you *monitor your knowledge* after reading in the textbook. The statements help you master the important concepts that are at the heart of the material by exercising your usage of the textbook terms and concepts in verbal statements of fact. With this strategy the student receives immediate feedback and, if wrong, where to go to figure out the right answer. It is a very effective learning strategy for its simplicity. Try some of the Programmed Review after your textbook reading and see how well you do!

Directions: After active reading of each chapter or chapter section of the text, close the book and keep it nearby. Obtain a sheet of paper and find in this study guide to the Programmed Review for that chapter. Using the paper to cover the answer written immediately below each statement, pull it down the printed page to reveal just the statement and nothing more. Then write down an appropriate response that makes the statement a fact; do not skip over these statements passively or automatically "read in" the answers below each statement. After writing down your response, move your cover sheet down the page to reveal the answer. If you are correct, move on to the next statement. If you are incorrect, then immediately turn to the page in the textbook given to the right of the answer to review the given concept.

Multiple Choice Questions

After studying the textbook, familiarizing yourself with the major concepts, and completing the Programmed Review, you are ready to test your general knowledge of the chapter material. The Multiple Choice questions are provided as another diagnostic tool to prepare for exams in the course. While it is recommended that you study the textbook in manageable sections rather than all in one sitting, the Multiple Choice section should be completed in one brief session. Take this test before moving on to sharpen your knowledge with the open-ended essay questions in the last two sections.

Multiple Choice questions come in two varieties: definitional/conceptual questions and application questions. The definitional/conceptual questions test your knowledge of the facts and definitions of concepts. The application questions help you determine how well you can apply your knowledge in everyday life. The answer key is given at the end of each chapter of the study guide along with the appropriate textbook page number for the answer to each question. It is recommended that you use this information to evaluate your understanding and return to the text to review areas which need more study.

Integrative Questions

A higher level of knowledge is the level of integration at which individual facts and concepts are synthesized and interrelated to strengthen your command of the material. Integrative questions require you to discover the deeper meaning and relationships among major topics within each chapter and even across chapters. These questions and the Evaluative Questions in the last section are not tests. They should be considered learning exercises because your answer is likely to be uniquely yours, appropriately based on your own understanding of the material.

Evaluative Questions

Perhaps an even deeper level of understanding is the ability to assess and critically evaluate the issues and concepts that you have learned from careful study of the textbook. The Evaluative Questions will focus your critical thinking skills on selected topics. Like the Integrative Questions, there are no specific answers except those found in your careful study of the textbook. Exercise your knowledge by considering each question one at a time. Then write out your answer using the appropriate terms and showing good reasoning. Be sure to *support* all of your assertions with information presented in the textbook. When you have finished writing your essay answer, go back into the textbook and evaluate the answer for yourself. While you assess the goodness of your answer you will discover yourself learning even more.

We are enthusiastic about your success in this personality class and we encourage you to study effectively by making good use of the learning activities in this study guide. You can even use these same strategies in your other classes because the are effective methods of learning in college. By exercising and elaborating your growing knowledge of the theories, applications, and assessment of personality psychology, as well as knowledge of the relevant research, you will be prepared to demonstrate to your instructor what you know with confidence. More importantly, you will improve your general learning skills and you will become better prepared to apply your knowledge of personality in your life and career. Best wishes for learning!

T. L. W.
J. M. B.

Chapter 1

What Is Personality?

The Person and the Situation

Defining Personality

Six Approaches to Personality

Personality and Culture

The Study of Personality: Theory, Application, Assessment, and Research

Learning Objectives

1. State whether behavior is influenced by the environment or reflects contributions by the individual. Explain why the situation is important to personality psychologists.
2. Define personality in your own words. State how psychologists answer the question, "What is personality?" Give examples to illustrate the two major parts of the definition of personality offered in the textbook.
3. Explain what is meant by the terms "intrapersonal processes" and "individual differences." Discuss the major factors that determine our individual character.
4. According to the six major approaches to personality, give six brief answers to the question, "What are the sources of consistent behavior and intrapersonal processes for the individual?" List by name and distinguish the six major approaches to personality.
5. Using either aggression or depression as an example, interpret the behavior pattern according to each of the major approaches to personality. Briefly state what these approaches would say about consistent feelings of guilt, panic attacks, and happiness.

6. Discuss the role culture plays in personality, including the distinction between individualistic and collectivist cultures. Using your own examples, illustrate how behaviors can take on different meanings depending on the culture.
7. List four components of the study of personality that are necessary for a complete understanding of the topic. For any two of the six approaches to personality, discuss how these components combine to help us understand personality constructs.
8. State the specific goals of personality theories. Describe three issues theorists wrestle with related to the nature of human personality and state how most psychologists think about each issue.
9. Discuss two ways in which personality psychologists use theories in their work, including the variety of applications and assessments from the six approaches to personality. Give two reasons why psychologists conduct personality research.

Important Concepts

personality (p. 2)
intrapersonal processes (p. 4)
individual differences (p. 4)
psychoanalytic approach (p. 5)
biological approach (p. 5)
cognitive approach (p. 5)
trait approach (p. 5)
humanistic approach (p. 5)
conscious versus unconscious (p. 14)

InfoTrac *Search terms:*

behavioral/social learning approach (p. 5)
individualistic culture (p. 11)
collectivist culture (p. 11)
determinism (p. 14)

Programmed Review

Many psychologists concern themselves with how people *typically* respond to _____ .

environmental demands p. 2

The author of the textbook defines personality as consistent ______ and intrapersonal processes originating within the individual.

behavior patterns p. 4

________ include all the emotional, motivational, and cognitive processes that go on inside the individual.

Intrapersonal processes p. 4

The _______ approach argues that people's unconscious minds are largely responsible for personality differences.

psychoanalytic p. 5

Behavioral/social learning theorists explain consistent behavior patterns as the result of _______ and expectations.

conditioning p. 5

The _______ approach looks at differences in the way people process information.

cognitive p. 5

Psychologists who take the behavioral/social learning approach to personality would suggest that aggressive behavior is learned because it has been ______ .

rewarded p. 7

The humanistic approach to personality suggests that problems like aggressive behavior result when something interferes with ______ processes.

natural growth p. 7

How you respond to a situation is a function of how you interpret it. This is a basic argument of the ______ approach to personality.

cognitive p. 8

Biological personality psychologists point to research that suggests some people inherit a _______ susceptibility to depression.

genetic p. 9

Most theorists presented in the textbook come from research in _______ cultures.

individualistic p. 11

Included in ______ are psychotherapy, education, and behavior in the workplace.

applications p. 15

Regardless of the approach, assessment is about how we ______ personality.

measure p. 15

Multiple Choice Questions

1. When we look closely at the reactions of people to the same situation, we see
   a. that people are more alike than they are different.
   b. that characteristic differences between people begin to emerge.
   c. evidence that most people behave in typical ways.
   d. each individual's personality is overwhelmed by the demands of the situation.

2. Which of the following questions would a personality psychologist ask?
   a. Why are some people prone to addiction?
   b. How can the success of college students be predicted?
   c. Why do some people help in traumatic situations while others don't?
   d. all of the above

3. Personality researchers use the term *individual differences* to refer to
   a. the different behavior patterns individuals display across time.
   b. the interpersonal processes that originate within the individual.
   c. the consistent behavior patterns individuals display across situations.
   d. fluctuations in behavior patterns for individual situations.

4. When she is home, Susan is very well behaved and polite. But Susan's mother is troubled when she learns that her daughter is rude and unkind at school. According to the psychoanalytic approach, Susan's behavior
   a. can be identified along a continuum of personality characteristics.
   b. is the result of unconscious mental activity.
   c. results from conditioning and expectations.
   d. is a reaction to changing feelings of self-acceptance.

5. Refer to Question #4 above. Psychologists who adhere to the trait approach to personality would say Susan's behavior
   a. can be identified along a continuum of personality characteristics.
   b. is the result of unconscious mental activity.
   c. results from conditioning and expectations.
   d. is a reaction to changing feelings of self-acceptance.

6. A personality psychologist who focuses on the stable patterns of aggressive behavior in schoolchildren that may be related to genetic predispositions follows the

   a. psychoanalytic approach.
   b. biological approach.
   c. humanistic approach.
   d. behavioral/social learning approach.

7. George believes that aggressive behavior in his coworkers is an expression of frustration that results from unsatisfied basic needs. George believes in the

   a. psychoanalytic approach.
   b. biological approach.
   c. behavioral/social learning approach.
   d. humanistic approach.

8. Which of the following approaches has focused on the way people learn from watching role models?

   a. psychoanalytic approach
   b. biological approach
   c. behavioral/social learning approach
   d. humanistic approach

9. The approach to personality that explains aggressive behavior as unconscious impulses turned outward on other people is the

   a. psychoanalytic approach.
   b. trait approach.
   c. behavioral/social learning approach.
   d. cognitive approach.

10. To explain depression, trait theorists would be most likely to focus on

   a. identifying persons prone to depression.
   b. the genetic susceptibility individuals have toward depression.
   c. the unconscious feelings of anger within people.
   d. how people interpret a world that seems uncontrollable.

11. Which of the following approaches to personality explains depression by how situations are perceived and interpreted?

   a. psychoanalytic approach
   b. behavioral/social learning approach
   c. cognitive approach
   d. trait approach

12. Mary has been diagnosed as clinically depressed. She has suffered with changing moods and reduced energy and interest for many years. Her therapist has assessed her condition and made a plan for her treatment. According to the psychoanalytic approach, Mary's depression is most likely

    a. due to a malfunction of the brain.
    b. predictable from earlier episodes of depression.
    c. a result of feelings of hostility turned inward.
    d. due to low self-esteem.

13. For people who are depressed, a psychologist following the behavioral/social learning approach to personality would probably examine

    a. what depressed persons say about themselves.
    b. the best predictors of emotional level.
    c. the genetic susceptibility to depression.
    d. the environment surrounding the depressed person.

14. Which of these is *not* a characteristic of an individual in a collectivist culture?

    a. success identified with personal achievement
    b. success identified with group accomplishments
    c. cooperation
    d. dependency

15. Suppose you meet a new person on campus from a culture different from your own. You soon discover that your new friend has difficulty understanding what you mean by "self-esteem." You conclude that your friend probably comes from

    a. an individualistic culture.
    b. a collectivist culture.
    c. a nonindustrial culture.
    d. a large family.

16. Of the four components necessary for the study of personality, which is characterized by inventories, tests, and direct observations?

    a. theory
    b. assessment
    c. research
    d. application

17. Of the following approaches, which ignores inherited (genetic) influences the most?

    a. cognitive
    b. biological
    c. trait
    d. psychoanalytic

18. Among the applications of the study of personality, _______ applies personality theory to address personal and social needs.

    a. assessment
    b. education
    c. hypothesis-testing
    d. psychotherapy

19. While the psychology of Freud and the views of Skinner represent extreme positions on the conscious versus unconscious determinants issue, _______ psychologists now recognize how much information is processed below awareness.

    a. behavioral/social learning
    b. cognitive
    c. biological
    d. humanistic

20. Of the many approaches to personality, which represents an extreme position on the issue in psychology of free will versus determinism?

    a. psychoanalytic approach
    b. trait approach
    c. humanistic approach
    d. cognitive approach

21. To apply personality research to practical concerns, behavioral psychologists

    a. try to change the way people process information.
    b. design environments to increase the frequency of desired behavior.
    c. identify characteristics of individuals in the workplace.
    d. help people develop their self-concept.

22. Asking people to respond to ambiguous stimuli is an example of ________ in the study of personality.

    a. research
    b. application
    c. assessment
    d. theory

Integrative Questions

1. What is the generally agreed-upon answer to the question of whether our behavior is shaped by the situation or by the kind of person we are? Give three reasons for the answer to this question. (2)

2. Write a two-paragraph short story about a situation in which individuals react differently to the same event. In the story give examples of reactions that are the result of situational factors and distinguish these from reactions that are the result of intrapersonal processes. (2-4)

3. It is stated in the text that each of the major theories of personality can be placed into one of the six general approaches. Turn to the Table of Contents in the textbook and create a list of the major theories by name, categorizing them by approach. (4-5)

4. Think of a person you know who is aggressive. State in your own words how each of the six general approaches to personality explain that person's behavior. (6-8)

5. For each of the three dichotomies that follow, close your textbook and draw a line representing a continuum with poles indicating the two extreme positions for each dichotomy. Then place each of the six general approaches to personality along each continuum according to your understanding and check your work (see p. 13). If an approach makes no distinction, then place it in the center of the continuum. (13-15)

   (1) genetic versus environmental influences emphasized
   (2) conscious versus unconscious determinants of behavior emphasized
   (3) free will versus determinism as underlying assumption

6. Give an example of one kind of application of personality theory from two different approaches of your own choosing. In what ways is the application different across the two approaches? In what ways are they similar? (15)

7. State the major purposes of research in personality psychology. Contrast the kinds of questions that would be addressed by research within three of the different approaches to personality. (15-16)

Evaluative Questions

1. Do psychologists agree on a single definition of personality? What should psychologists look at to study personality? State one advantage and one disadvantage of differing theoretical viewpoints in the field of personality. (3-4)

2. Restate briefly the story of the blind men and the elephant. Why is the blind men analogy only partially applicable to the six approaches to personality? (5)

3. Consider how each of the six general approaches to personality would explain unwanted aggressive behavior in an adolescent. From the basic tenets of each approach, which of the approaches holds the most promise for eliminating the aggressive behavior? Explain your answer. (6-8)

4. Each of the six approaches to personality gives a different explanation for depression. State three possible answers to the question of which approach is correct in explaining the causes of depression. (8-10)

5. What does it mean to say that personalities exist within a cultural context? Give your own reasons for why culture is important in understanding personality. Which of the six general approaches is best suited for explaining culture's role in personality? (11)

6. List the three theoretical issues faced by personality psychologists. Give your own personal belief about each issue and state how most psychologists think about each one. Has your personal view of any of these issues changed since starting college? Given these issues, does the study of personality meet the goals of theory, in your own estimation? (13-15)

Answers to Multiple Choice Questions

1. b, 2
2. d, 3
3. c, 4
4. b, 5
5. a, 5
6. b, 7
7. d, 7
8. c, 7
9. a, 6
10. a, 9
11. c, 10
12. c, 9
13. d, 10
14. a, 11
15. b, 11
16. b, 12
17. a, 13
18. d, 15
19. b, 14
20. c, 14
21. b, 15
22. c, 15

Chapter 2

Personality Research Methods

The Hypothesis-Testing Approach

The Case Study Method

Statistical Analysis of Data

Personality Assessment

Learning Objectives

1. Distinguish among speculation, expert opinion, and empirical research as ways of understanding personality. State how the hypothesis-testing approach makes possible strong evidence in support of a theory.
2. Describe the four general steps of the hypothesis-testing approach. Define and state the distinction between theories and hypotheses.
3. Define with an example each of the two characteristics of good theories. Explain how psychologists test the adequacy of a theory, including with what kinds of questions they begin their research.
4. Give an example of an independent and a dependent variable. State how each variable is used in experimental research. Identify each of these variables in research hypotheses.
5. Explain the difference in the research process with manipulated and nonmanipulated independent variables. State the kinds of conclusions that can be drawn from research using each of these kinds of independent variables.
6. Discuss under what circumstances personality researchers make predictions about data, including how a theory is tested from predictions. State the circumstances under which a researcher should replicate a study.

7. Give an example of the case study method indicating who is studied with this method and how the data are collected. List four different occasions in history when the case study method was a useful tool in personality research.
8. Describe three limitations to the case study method. State four occasions when the case study method is useful in studying personality.
9. State what it means to say research results are statistically significant. Give the role probability plays in statistical decisions. Describe two situations in which one would and would not conclude statistical significance.
10. Identify the appropriate use of the correlation coefficient. Discuss the possible outcomes of a correlational analysis, including the direction and strength (interpretation) of the correlation coefficient.
11. Give examples of what is meant by "personality assessment" from areas of psychology in which assessment is necessary.
12. Explain how one distinguishes a good personality test from a bad one. Discuss the concept of reliability and give an example of a measure that is not reliable based on a test-retest reliability coefficient.
13. Explain how one determines if a test score measures what it is designed to measure. Discuss the concept of validity and explain the difference between predictive validity and construct validity using an example of a hypothetical construct.
14. Distinguish among face, congruent, and discriminant validity. State the purpose of establishing each of these kinds of validity. Discuss and give an example of behavioral validation.

Important Concepts

expert opinion (p. 18)
empirical research (p. 19)
theory (p. 20)
parsimonious (p. 20)
hypothesis (p. 20)
independent variable (p. 23)
dependent variable (p. 23)
interaction (p. 24)
manipulated independent variable (p. 25)
nonmanipulated independent variable (p. 26)
replication (p. 28)
statistical significance (p. 32)
positive correlation (p. 33)
negative correlation (p. 33)
reliability (p. 35)
validity (p. 36)
test-retest reliability (p. 36)
internal consistency (p. 36)
predictive validity (p. 37)
congruent validity (p. 37)
construct validity (p. 37)
face validity (p. 37)
behavioral validation (p. 38)
discriminant validity (p. 38)

InfoTrac *Search terms:*

statistical hypothesis-testing (p. 19)
case study method (p. 28)
correlation coefficient (p. 32)
hypothetical constructs (p. 37)

Programmed Review

Because theories alone only provide part of the picture of personality, most psychologists want strong evidence from _______ .

empirical research p. 19

Most personality research begins with a ______ .

theory p. 20

Unless a theory can generate _______ , it may be of little use to scientists.

testable hypotheses p. 20

A formal prediction about the relationship between two or more variables is more commonly called a _______ .

hypothesis p. 20

The variable that determines how the groups in an experiment are divided or specified is the _______ variable.

independent p. 23

When the effects of one independent variable depends on the level of another independent variable, the result is called _______ .

an interaction p. 24

The use of _______ variables is required when an independent variable exists without the experimenter's intervention.

nonmanipulated p. 26

One way to deal with the problem of assuming that one significant finding provides reliable evidence of a phenomenon is through ______ .

replication p. 28

In the case study method, instead of reporting the results of statistical analysis, the investigators describe their _______ of what the person did and what it means.

impressions p. 28

One problem with the case study method is the problem of ______ from any one case to other people.

generalizing p. 29

Researchers typically rely on a statistical significance level of ______ .

.05 or 5% p. 32

The ______ is the appropriate statistic when we want to understand the relationship between two measures.

correlation coefficient p. 32

The value of the correlation coefficient can range from _______ .

1.00 to -1.00 p. 33

A test has good _______ when it measures consistently.

reliability p. 35

A test has _______ when all of the items on the test measure the same concept.

internal consistency p. 36

The extent to which a test measures what it is designed to measure is called _______ .

validity p. 36

Demonstrating that a test accurately measures the test taker's level on a hypothetical construct establishes the test's _______ validity.

construct p. 37

When a test appears to be measuring the hypothetical construct it is supposed to measure, then the test has good _______ .

face validity p. 37

_______ validity refers to the extent to which test scores do not correlate with scores from tests or measures of theoretically unrelated constructs.

Discriminant p. 38

Multiple Choice Questions

1. Personality theorists who use empirical research to support their theory make use of

   a. sophisticated speculation about patterns of behavior.
   b. expert opinion almost exclusively.
   c. rigorous methods to collect data and test hypotheses.
   d. direct observation of people in their natural surroundings.

2. In what order do researchers take steps to discover the nature of personality?

   a. Generate hypotheses, evaluate data, speculate
   b. Generate hypotheses, collect data, evaluate data
   c. Collect data, evaluate data, speculate
   d. Speculate, collect data, generate hypotheses

3. Most personality researchers today are unlike Sigmund Freud in that

   a. they speculate about where behaviors come from.
   b. modern researchers use case studies to understand personality.
   c. they typically work with theories that are more narrow in their application.
   d. they mostly work with theories that have broader applications.

4. Most of the research reported in your textbook began with a ______ from which predictions were derived and tested.

   a. hypothesis
   b. behavioral phenomenon
   c. speculation
   d. theory

5. A good theory is parsimonious, meaning that it is characteristically

   a. provable.
   b. useful.
   c. simple.
   d. testable.

6. You are studying the immediate effects of alcohol on people's feelings of well-being. Which of the following could be the dependent variable in this study?

   a. level of alcohol in the blood
   b. score on a measure of well-being
   c. amount of alcohol consumed within one hour prior to test
   d. either a or c

7. By randomly assigning research participants to treatment conditions, personality researchers can assume that all of the different life experiences of the participants

   a. even out.
   b. become the same through the use of manipulated variables.
   c. are included in the hypothesis.
   d. start out exactly the same.

8. A subject variable, which is a characteristic of research participants, is also known as

   a. a hypothesis.
   b. a manipulated independent variable.
   c. a nonmanipulated independent variable.
   d. a personality assessment.

9. Understanding personality with an in-depth evaluation of a single individual or group of people is better known as

   a. the hypothesis-testing method.
   b. the experimental approach.
   c. the correlation coefficient.
   d. the case study method.

10. If the difference in a measured behavior is so small between experimental groups that it could be caused by a chance fluctuation, then we say

    a. the result reached statistical significance.
    b. the result was reliable between groups.
    c. the result failed to reach statistical significance.
    d. the result established a cause-and-effect relationship.

11. Which of the following describes the relationship between your checking account balance and the amount of money you withdraw on several occasions?

    a. a perfect negative correlation
    b. a weak negative correlation
    c. a perfect negative correlation
    d. a strong positive correlation

12. Among the disadvantages of the case study method is

    a. the possibility of subjective judgments.
    b. the difficulty with determining relationships among variables.
    c. the difficulty of examining certain concepts experimentally.
    d. the problem of replicating a treatment.

13. Statistical tests of significance provide a yes or no answer to which question?

   a. Is there a correlation between variable X and variable Y?
   b. Does the treatment cause changes in behavior?
   c. Is the difference in the treatment conditions due to chance?
   d. none of the above

14. Which of the following is the strongest correlation coefficient?

   a. 0.89
   b. –0.98
   c. 0.00
   d. –0.05

15. Jack found in his study of self-esteem that the higher the self-esteem of the subjects in his sample, the less problems they had at work. Jack has found evidence for a

   a. cause of work-related satisfaction.
   b. statistically significant positive correlation.
   c. statistically significant negative correlation.
   d. none of the above

16. Which of the following is true about replication in experimental research?

   a. We often use different experimental methods to reach different conclusions.
   b. We deal with the problem of prediction versus hindsight by replicating the results of original research.
   c. We often use participant populations different from those used in the original research.
   d. We tend to explain effect after the data are in.

17. Which of the following is a problem of test validity?

   a. when test responses are dependent on recent events
   b. when test questions are vague
   c. when similar test responses cannot be obtained in a second testing
   d. when test responses do not reflect the hypothetical constructs being measured

18. Which of the following test-retest coefficients is the most acceptable?

   a. .35
   b. .60
   c. .05
   d. - .88

19. Jenny is conducting a study of the personality of eighth-graders and discovers from statistical analysis that her test's items are measuring more than one concept. Jenny's problem is one of

   a. internal consistency.
   b. reliability.
   c. statistical significance.
   d. predictive validity.

20. Good hypothetical constructs are

   a. actual events in the life experiences of individuals.
   b. explanations that underlie the structure of hypotheses and theories.
   c. inventions.
   d. typically dependent on one's intelligence level.

21. By just looking at the items of a test, researchers can determine the test's

   a. construct validity.
   b. face validity.
   c. discriminant validity.
   d. reliability.

22. When scores from a test correlate with other measures of the same construct, researchers can determine the test's

   a. congruent validity.
   b. face validity.
   c. construct validity.
   d. discriminant validity.

23. The method of behavioral validation allows researchers to predict relevant behavior from test scores to assist them in knowing the

   a. reliability of a test.
   b. construct validity of a test.
   c. face validity of a measure.
   d. statistical significance of a hypothesis.

Integrative Questions

1. Review what Ann Landers wrote to "Desperate in Dallas" and the others in the first paragraph of the text chapter. If you were to address the questions put to Ann with empirical research, then what would be the hypothesis to be tested in each of these cases? What variables would be considered in each? What results would you expect if Ann were correct in her answers? (18)

2. Develop a hypothesis of your own about why some students study more than others. Identify the independent and dependent variables in your hypothesis and briefly describe an experiment to test your hypothesis. What result do you expect? (23)

3. Contrast the empirical research method and the case study method as means of understanding personality. How do they compare in terms of their goals and the kinds of data collected in each? (19, 28)

4. Develop a sketch of a study of your own in which the correlation coefficient is the appropriate statistical test. From your example study, describe three possible outcomes of the test and what each outcome indicates about the variables in your example study. Give values for the correlation coefficient that reflect these three different outcomes. (32-33)

5. Discuss the concepts of test-retest reliability and internal consistency, contrasting their purpose and the ways in which each concept is measured and indexed. (36)

6. Give an example of a personality test that has high construct validity but low face validity. What does discriminant validity tell you about a test measure? Can there be congruent validity without discriminant validity? (37-38)

Evaluative Questions

1. What makes a theory good? Briefly evaluate each of the six general approaches to personality that you learned in Chapter 1 with respect to the characteristics of good theories. (4-6, 20)

2. Why do you think it was stated in the text that theories are never proven or disproven? State the advantages and disadvantages to testing hypotheses without a larger theory from which they are derived. In what research context is atheoretical research meaningful? (19-22)

3. Suppose a researcher came to the following conclusion from a study: "The severity of a patient's psychosis makes them less likely to seek treatment." From what you know about manipulated versus nonmanipulated independent variables, specify why the conclusion cannot be valid. (24-26)

4. Can we come to understand personality using the case study method alone? Does the method have a place in personality research? Justify your answer. (28-29)

5. The textbook author states that there is no such thing as a perfect experiment. In your own words, give the author's reasoning for making this statement. Do you agree or disagree? What is the solution to the imperfect nature of research? (27)

6. Sigmund Freud made careful observations of his neurotic patients, and from his notes he formulated the basis of his psychoanalytic theory. Then Freud applied his theoretical concepts to everyday psychology and attempted to explain everything about human personality. From a modern scientist's perspective, what is the major difficulty with such an encompassing theory? (27-28)

7. When we consider the reliability and the validity of a personality test, why is the question *not* whether the test has either of these characteristics or not? Explain whether it is possible for a test to have face validity, congruent validity, and discriminant validity and still have questionable construct validity. (35-38)

Answers to Multiple Choice Questions

1. c, 19
2. b, 20
3. c, 20
4. d, 20
5. c, 20
6. b, 23
7. a, 24
8. c, 26
9. d, 28
10. c, 32
11. c, 33
12. a, 29
13. d, 32
14. b, 33
15. c, 33
16. c, 27
17. d, 36
18. b, 36
19. a, 36
20. c, 37
21. b, 37
22. a, 37
23. b, 38

Chapter 3

The Psychoanalytic Approach

Freudian Theory, Application, and Assessment

Learning Objectives

1. Give three examples of ways in which Freudian theory has influenced our culture. Tell the story of how Freud discovered the unconscious.
2. Describe the topographic model proposed by Freud. State the divisions of the human personality in the topographic model and give an example of material from each.
3. Describe the structural model of personality proposed by Freud. Define each division and state the objective of each structure and the principles on which each rests. Explain where in the topographic model each of the three parts of the structural model can be found.

4. Give the name and meaning behind each of the two major categories of instinct. Explain how psychic energy and each of these drives are involved in psychological functions, according to Freud.
5. List by name each of the Freudian ego defense mechanisms and give a definition and example for each. Identify the most and least successful defense mechanisms.
6. Describe each of the stages of psychosexual development. State the tenets upon which Freud's theory of personality development rests. Give the approximate ages and an example of a fixation related to each stage.
7. Describe the various techniques for getting at unconscious material. Specify the importance and function of dreams according to Freud. State the ways in which the unconscious is revealed in projective tests, free association, and in everyday life.
8. Discuss Freud's system of psychotherapy to treat psychological disorders. Explain the basis of psychoanalysis and describe the techniques used to get and interpret unconscious material.
9. Explain the role of resistance and the roles of transference and countertransference in the therapy process. State the optimal outcome of treatment using psychoanalysis.
10. Discuss the use of projective tests as a means of personality assessment. Give the names and a description of three projective tests. State the criticisms that have been made and potential misuses of projective tests.
11. Indicate the strengths of the psychoanalytic approach to personality, including the benefits for which we can give Freud credit and Freud's place in history.
12. Identify three general criticisms that can be made of Freud's theory of personality. Explain why some argue that Freud's ideas do not make a valuable scientific theory.

Important Concepts

hysteria (p. 42)
topographical model (p. 45)
conscious (p. 45)
preconscious (p. 45)
unconscious (p. 46)
structural model (p. 46)
wish fulfillment (p. 46)
id (p. 46)
pleasure principle (p. 46)
reality principle (p. 46)
ego (p. 47)
superego (p. 47)
thanatos (p. 48)
neurotic anxiety (p. 49)
repression (p. 49)
sublimation (p. 49)
displacement (p. 50)
projection (p. 51)
reaction formation (p. 51)
intellectualization (p. 51)
erogenous zone (p. 51)
oral stage (p. 53)
anal stage (p. 53)
fixation (p. 53)

(continued on next page)

phallic stage (p. 54)
castration anxiety (p. 54)
penis envy (p. 55)
latency stage (p. 55)
genital stage (p. 55)
manifest content (p. 56)
latent content (p. 56)
free association (p. 57)
Thematic Apperception Test (p. 63)
Human Figure Drawing Test (p. 63)
projective tests (p. 57)
Freudian slips (p. 58)
symbolic behavior (p. 58)
psychoanalysis (p. 59)
resistance (p. 61)
transference (p. 61)
countertransference (p. 61)

InfoTrac *Search terms:*

unconscious (p. 46)
libido (p. 48)
defense mechanisms (psychology) (p. 49)
denial (p. 50)
psychosexual development (p. 51)
Oedipus complex (p. 54)
dreams-interpretation (p. 56)
hypnosis (p. 58)
Rorschach inkblot test (p. 62)

Programmed Review

Most people in this culture freely accept the idea that behavior is sometimes influenced by an ______ part of the mind.

unconscious p. 42

People who suffer from ______ display a variety of symptoms such as blindness, the inability to use an arm, or loss of language.

hysteria p. 42

Three parts of the personality that differ in terms of their level of awareness make up the _______ model in Freudian theory.

topographic p. 45

Freud described the conscious and preconscious as merely the tip of the ______ .

iceberg p. 46

The primary job of the ______ is to satisfy id impulses in a manner that takes reality into consideration.

ego p. 46

People who suffer from an ever-present feeling of shame or guilt suffer from ______ .

moral anxiety p. 48

The techniques the ego uses to deal with unwanted thoughts and desires are collectively known as ______ .

defense mechanisms p. 49

The defense mechanism upon which the whole structure of psychoanalysis rests is the one known as ______ .

repression p. 49

One defense mechanism that is successful, productive, and adaptive is ______ .

sublimation p. 49

Removing the emotional content from an unwanted thought or t ıterial is the defense mechanism called ______ .

intellectualization p. 51

The first stage of personality development according to Freud is the ______ stage.

oral p. 53

Boys develop ______ when they fear that their father will discover their incestuous desires for their mother.

castration anxiety p. 54

The time before puberty is a time when sexual desires abate and is called the ______ .

latency stage p. 55

Freud believed that ______ are the "royal road to the unconscious" and represent the things and events we desire.

dreams p. 56

Misstatements that reveal underlying unconscious feelings are called ______ .

Freudian slips p. 57

Freud's system of psychotherapy is known as ______ .

psychoanalysis p. 59

When a patient declares to their therapist that the therapy isn't helping and they want to stop treatment, the patient is developing a necessary part of therapy called ______ .

resistance p. 61

When a patient receiving psychoanalysis displaces emotions for other people on the therapist, the patient is said to be showing ______ .

transference p. 61

When a therapist presents a patient with ambiguous stimuli, he or she is probably using an assessment known as a ______ .

projective test p. 61

The assessment known as the Rorschach test consists of ten cards, each containing nothing more than a _______ .

blot of ink p. 62

One criticism of Freud's case study data is that his patients did not represent ______ .

typical adults p. 68

Multiple Choice Questions

1. Which is an example of an everyday concept that comes from Freud?
    a. denial
    b. unconscious
    c. repression
    d. all of the above

2. The life instinct or sexual drive to which Freud attributed most of our behaviors is called

   a. the structural model.
   b. neurotic anxiety.
   c. libido.
   d. id.

3. The neurologist in Paris who demonstrated hypnosis to Freud was

   a. Breuer.
   b. Charcot.
   c. Jung.
   d. Anna O.

4. Which of the following is true about hypnosis?

   a. Freud always made hypnosis a large part of therapy.
   b. After using hypnosis for a time, Freud began using it exclusively.
   c. Hypnosis is not a real phenomenon because hypnotized people are faking it.
   d. Freud grew disillusioned by hypnosis as a treatment and turned to free association.

5. Which of the following is true about Freud's early work?

   a. His work was opposed by the academic and medical communities.
   b. After some initial success, Freud's techniques failed to work and his reputation soon suffered.
   c. Freud never spoke of his views of infantile sexuality because he feared opposition.
   d. He enjoyed much acceptance from his professional colleagues from the start.

6. Memories of past events and other information that is easily retrievable comprise the

   a. conscious.
   b. preconscious.
   c. unconscious.
   d. id.

7. The id, ego, and superego are three parts of the ______ model of personality.

   a. topographic
   b. iceberg
   c. structural
   d. libido

8. Freud said the actions of the ego were characterized as following which principle?

   a. pleasure principle
   b. ethical principle
   c. morality principle
   d. reality principle

9. If the superego could talk, which of the following would it most likely say?

   a. "I am so mad that I could bash in that guy's skull!"
   b. "Why not tell the person to respect the privacy of others?"
   c. "I want to have sex with that person right now."
   d. "Now, you know that you don't hate anyone."

10. Lisa is a married woman who sees her doctor whenever she has the slightest symptom of a physical problem because she is attracted to him. It is most probably her __________ that decides to behave this way.

    a. id
    b. ego
    c. superid
    d. superego

11. Sexually motivated behaviors include both those with obvious erotic content and

    a. just about anything that leads to pleasure.
    b. those with obvious self-destruction content.
    c. instincts to return to the earth through death.
    d. those sexual behaviors we hide from society or deny to ourselves.

12. When we see our own unwanted thoughts and undesirable impulses in other people, we are using the defense mechanism called

    a. displacement.
    b. reaction formation.
    c. intellectualization.
    d. projection.

13. Repression is an __________ effort by the ego to push or keep threatening material out of consciousness.

    a. occasional
    b. organic
    c. active
    d. irrational

14. Jim feels a strong desire to view pornographic material, but instead he becomes a minister who preaches self-control and assists his congregation in their efforts to live pure lives and avoid sexually explicit media. Jim's ego is defending through

    a. displacement.
    b. sublimation.
    c. reaction formation.
    d. denial.

15. One way to think of the concept of fixation is that fixation occurs during development when

    a. we use defense mechanisms to deal with unconscious sexual and aggressive impulses.
    b. children leave behind some psychic energy tied up in resolving a crisis.
    c. the rewards in the environment control our behaviors.
    d. all of the above

16. Little Timmy is extremely jealous whenever his mommy and daddy kiss and show affection. Timmy wants to get kisses from his mommy. Little Timmy is in the __________ stage of psychosexual development.

    a. oral
    b. anal
    c. phallic
    d. genital

17. George is an adult who chews on his fingernails whenever he is nervous. Sometimes he chews gum instead since he gave up smoking. George is most likely fixated at which psychosexual stage of development?

    a. oral
    b. anal
    c. phallic
    d. genital

18. According to Freud, which of the following is a healthy result of castration anxiety in males?

    a. repression of sexual desires for opposite sex people
    b. strong moral anxiety
    c. a powerful superego
    d. identification with the same-sex parent

19. Which of the following techniques for getting at unconscious material was characterized by Freud as a type of wish fulfillment?

    a. free association
    b. Freudian slips
    c. symbolic behavior
    d. dreams

20. The use of ___________ requires an individual to respond to ambiguous stimuli.

    a. free association
    b. projective tests
    c. dream analysis
    d. hypnosis

21. Clients in therapy who claim they forgot their regular appointment with the therapist could be displaying a form of

    a. resistance.
    b. symbolic behavior.
    c. reaction formation.
    d. denial.

22. Sally is undergoing psychoanalysis for the treatment of her psychological problems. She is given a set of cards on which ambiguous pictures of people are displayed. Sally's therapist is using the

    a. Rorschach inkblot test.
    b. Thematic Apperception Test.
    c. free association test.
    d. Human Figure Drawing Test.

23. Of the following defense mechanisms, which do personality psychologists make use of when testing personality?

    a. sublimation
    b. displacement
    c. intellectualization
    d. projection

24. With respect to the Rorschach inkblot test, Dawes (1994) has suggested that it is not a valid test of

    a. anything.
    b. personality.
    c. id impulses.
    d. projection.

Integrative Questions

1. Write the story of how Freud discovered the unconscious in your own words. In the story give examples of hysteria and the use of hypnosis and free association. (42)

2. Describe the component structures in Freud's structural model. Explain where each structure fits within the topographic model. State the kinds of anxiety that result from lack of control of each of the three structures of personality. (45-48)

3. Make a list of the defense mechanisms proposed by Freud. For each mechanism give an example from your own life or someone you know that has used the defense mechanism to reduce or avoid anxiety. (49-51)

4. State the similarities and differences between each of the following pairs of defense mechanisms:

    a. repression and denial (49-50)
    b. sublimation and displacement (49-50)
    c. reaction formation and projection (51)

5. Describe each of the stages of psychosexual development in order, giving the approximate age when each stage takes place and an example of a fixation at each stage. Choose one fixation and give an example of adult behavior that results from it. (51-55)

6. State how the process of free association, taking projective tests, and making Freudian slips are alike. In other words, what is the fundamental idea behind each of these as ways of getting at unconscious material? (57)

7. Describe the series of events in a typical course of treatment using psychoanalysis. What must take place for the patient's treatment to be considered a success? (61)

8. Discuss and compare the three types of projective tests described in the text. Under what circumstances would one type of test be used rather than another? (61-65)

Evaluative Questions

1. Why is it said that Freud's approach to treating psychological disorders was radical? Why was it not accepted by other physicians of his day? Given what you know about personality research methods from Chapter 2, evaluate Freud's theory and methods of assessment. In other words, if Freud's approach was new today, would it be any more accepted than it was then? (42-43, 56-59)

2. There have been many approaches to mental functioning and models of mental structure in the past 100 years in psychology. Why do you suppose Freud thought of the mind as forces pulling and pushing at one another? Do you agree with this conceptualization of the mind and structure of personality? Why? (46)

3. What do you think of Freud's statement that dreams are the "royal road to the unconscious"? Give evidence from your own dreams to explain why you agree or disagree. Evaluate Freud's dream theory in terms of the validity of the interpretation of symbolic representations in dreams. (56)

4. Of all the various ways to get at unconscious material, with which do you think the most material can be uncovered? Support your answer and state how the psychoanalyst uses the technique. (56-59)

5. State the ultimate goal of psychoanalysis. How does the therapist know treatment has been a success? How does the outcome of treatment fit Freud's overall approach to personality? (59-61)

6. Summarize each critical point about the use of projective tests given in the textbook. Do you agree these are revealing of one's personality? Clearly state your reasoning in terms of the key assumptions underlying their use for assessment. (61-65)

7. Given what you know about Freud's life history, what aspects of his approach to personality reflect his experience and the times in which he lived? If Freud had been a woman, all other things being equal, discuss how you think his approach to personality would have been different. (66-68)

Answers to Multiple Choice Questions

1. d, 42
2. c, 48
3. b, 42
4. d, 43
5. a, 43-45
6. b, 45
7. c, 46
8. d, 46
9. d, 47
10. b, 47
11. a, 48
12. d, 51
13. c, 49
14. b, 49
15. b, 53
16. c, 54
17. a, 53
18. d, 54
19. d, 56
20. b, 57
21. a, 58
22. b, 63
23. d, 62
24. a, 65

Chapter 4

The Freudian Approach

Relevant Research

Dream Interpretation

Defense Mechanisms

Humor

Hypnosis

Learning Objectives

1. Summarize general criticisms of Freud's approach to personality. List some aspects of Freud's theory that have been examined by research.
2. State why Freud examined and interpreted his patients' dreams. Discuss the meaning of dream content, according to Freud, and his explanation of the recurrent dream.
3. Discuss Freud's response to the challenge of explaining *why* we dream. Specify the different kinds of sleep according to modern research. State the value of REM sleep and how it was demonstrated. Give research data in support of Freud's dream theory.
4. Give a definition of defense mechanisms according to Freud. State the defense mechanism considered to be the cornerstone of psychoanalysis and why it is.
5. Describe the methods and tests used to identify and measure defense mechanisms. Give some examples of defense mechanisms studied in the research literature.
6. Discuss the developmental and individual differences related to defense mechanisms. For several defense mechanisms, specify the age at which they manifest themselves. Define the meaning of defensive style.
7. State the significance of humor for Freud and discuss his theory of humor. Explain the relationship between humor and both aggression and psychic tension.

8. Summarize the research findings on Freud's theory of humor. Specify the predictions made by Freudian theory with respect to humor and whether these predictions are supported by the relevant research.
9. Define hypnosis. Contrast a psychoanalytic description of hypnotic phenomena with a social-cognitive description of these. State which position most hypnosis practitioners take.
10. Describe the approach to hypnosis known as neodissociation theory. State the research evidence in support of this theory.
11. Define posthypnotic amnesia and hypnotic responsiveness. Give three variables that affect hypnotic responsiveness. Describe the psychoanalytic explanations for these phenomena and give one argument against the Freudian approach for each.

Important Concepts

dream content (p. 73)
recurrent dream (p. 76)
rebound effect (p. 77)
paradoxical sleep (p. 77)
repression (p. 78)
defense mechanism (p. 78)
projective test (p. 79)
identification (p. 80)
denial (p. 81)
projection (p. 81)
defensive style (p. 83)
sublimation (p. 83)
"tendentious" jokes (p. 84)
catharsis (p. 85)
hostile humor (p. 87)
level of tension (p. 88)
pain analgesia (p. 92)
automatic writing (p. 92)
neodissociation theory (p. 92)
posthypnotic amnesia (p. 93)
hypnotic responsiveness (p. 94)
absorption (p. 95)

InfoTrac *Search terms:*

REM sleep (p. 77)
repressed memory (p. 78)
hypnosis (p. 89)

Programmed Review

Freud sought validation of his theory through __________ rather than empirical experiments.

methods p. 72

In dream research, sometimes sleepers are awakened when __________ measures indicate they are probably dreaming.

physiological p. 73

REM sleep has been argued to be quite beneficial to the dreamer and is sometimes called _________ sleep.

paradoxical p. 77

One function of dreams that Freud maintained was that dreams provide a safe and healthy outlet for expressing unconscious ________ .

conflicts p. 77

Freud eventually identified the defense mechanism ________ as the cornerstone of psychoanalysis.

repression p. 78

By definition, we are not aware of the __________ different defense mechanisms identified by Freud's daughter, Anna Freud.

ten p. 78

Before the use of more sophisticated defense mechanisms, children most often use ________ as a defense mechanism.

denial p. 81

Freud was not concerned with "innocent" jokes; rather he was concerned with what he called _________ jokes.

"tendentious" p. 84

The term Freud gave for a reduction of tension through laughter and other emotional reactions was _________ .

catharsis p. 85

According to Freud, jokes like those that attack marriage or other institutions often have disguised _________ .

aggression or hostility p. 87

While often misunderstood, hypnosis carries a number of potentially useful _________ .

applications p. 90

According to one explanation of hypnosis, the _________ forms a new subsystem when a person is under hypnosis.

ego p. 91

Hypnosis researchers have asked participants to report their experience through "automatic writing" that is taken as evidence for a _________ observer that is aware of what's going on.

hidden p. 92

________ theories of hypnosis point out that a person cannot do under hypnosis what they would not do without it.

Socio-cognitive p. 92

When hypnosis participants are told they will not remember what has happened during hypnosis, the hypnotist is inducing _________ .

posthypnotic amnesia p. 93

Multiple Choice Questions

1. A scientific approach to personality requires
   a. more than faith in one theory over another.
   b. that theory fits our personal perceptions.
   c. some understanding of our own feelings and behaviors.
   d. keen insight.

2. A therapist who agrees with Freud would say that the content of our dreams reveals
   a. much useless information.
   b. unconscious conflicts and desires.
   c. implicit punishments.
   d. unacceptable ideas that are really acceptable.

3. In one dream research study, subjects were asked prior to sleep for two nights to dream about some current problem they had in their lives. When the participants were awakened during the night to report their dreams, the results showed
   a. people do not really dream about their current concerns.
   b. participants had trouble remembering their dreams just after waking.
   c. people dream more about their current concerns than other suggested topics.
   d. those who received suggestions had more disturbances in their sleep.

4. Some people claim to have dreams they have dreamed before, typically about falling or being chased. These dreams are often called

    a. paradoxical.
    b. conscious.
    c. recurrent.
    d. hypnotic.

5. Which is true about the characters in men's dreams?

    a. The number of male characters is equal to the number of female characters.
    b. The number of male and female characters is equal to the number in women's dreams.
    c. Men are more likely to dream about female characters than male characters.
    d. Men are more likely to dream about male characters than female characters.

6. Dreams take place during a kind of sleep called

    a. REM sleep.
    b. paradoxical sleep.
    c. non-REM sleep.
    d. both a and b

7. Donny has to go all night without sleep in order to finish his term project by the deadline. The next night the amount of REM sleep Donny receives is likely to increase due to the

    a. paradox of sleep.
    b. relaxation associated with having the term project finished.
    c. rebound effect.
    d. recurrent dream phenomenon.

8. According to recent research findings, REM sleep appears to be necessary to

    a. maintain one's mental health.
    b. guard against serious psychological disturbances.
    c. prepare us for dealing with anxiety-arousing events.
    d. all of the above

9. Most researchers investigating the defense mechanisms make use of which kind of personality assessment?

    a. inventories
    b. behavioral interviews
    c. projective tests
    d. free association

10. Each of us relies on some defense mechanisms more than others when our ego is threatened. Psychologists refer to these differences as differences in

    a. defensive style.
    b. ego strength.
    c. preferred id impulses.
    d. mental health.

11. Research has shown that most young people entering adulthood use the defense mechanism called identification to

    a. reduce feelings of hostility toward authority figures.
    b. make gender-appropriate mating selections.
    c. fend off feelings of inadequacy and helplessness.
    d. deny their own uniqueness and become members of a social group.

12. Which of the following defense mechanisms is said to protect the individual by attributing unacceptable thoughts to someone else?

    a. identification
    b. reaction formation
    c. denial
    d. projection

13. Which of the following is *false* about sexual jokes?

    a. Jokes are often tolerated when open discussions of sex are inappropriate.
    b. Most sexually oriented jokes contain a great deal of humor.
    c. Freud suggested we laugh at sexual jokes to reduce tension.
    d. Freud argued that the humor content of a sexual joke rarely justifies the laughter.

14. When researchers asked high school students to write funny captions to pictures,

    a. more young men responded with sexual captions than young women.
    b. the students gave a great deal of responses with aggressive and sexual themes.
    c. the word "mother" was used in the majority of responses.
    d. responses that suggested pain or violence were nearly completely absent.

15. With respect to humor and tension reduction, Freud suggested that a joke will be funnier when

    a. it is sexual than when it is hostile.
    b. less tension is experienced before the punch line.
    c. tension increases rapidly.
    d. more tension is experienced before the punch line.

16. The view that deeply hypnotized people experience a division of their consciousness is known as

    a. neodissociation theory.
    b. socio-cognitive theory.
    c. trance theory.
    d. neonatal theory.

17. When researchers told participants under hypnosis that their "hidden observer" would experience less pain, then the participants reported

    a. more pain.
    b. less pain.
    c. no change in pain.
    d. a loss of hypnotic responsiveness.

18. One method used to break through posthypnotic amnesia was

    a. telling participants that a lie detector indicates they were lying.
    b. showing participants a videotape of their hypnotic experience.
    c. encouraging participants to be honest.
    d. all of the above

19. In which of the following circumstances are people more responsive to hypnosis?

    a. when the situation is not defined as hypnosis
    b. when the participant has not been responsive to hypnosis in the past
    c. when the cooperation and trust of the participant is established
    d. both a and b

20. Which of the following majors probably has the greatest percentage of students who are responsive to hypnotic suggestion?

    a. biology major
    b. philosophy major
    c. nursing major
    d. theater major

21. Which of the following is *not* a variable that determines hypnotic responsiveness?

    a. motivation
    b. expectancy
    c. intelligence
    d. attitude

Integrative Questions

1. Summarize at least three general criticisms of Freud's approach to personality. What specific aspects of Freud's theory have been examined by research? Is all the research evidence in support of Freud's work? Explain. (71-96)

2. What do people dream about? Why do people dream? Give a psychoanalytic interpretation of the research findings on dreams in your answers. (73-76)

3. Give a description of your own of the defense mechanisms used by children and contrast them with those used by adults. Give examples of different individual differences in defense mechanisms. (80-84)

4. Try a small study in which you pick three friends and ask each of them to write down their three favorite jokes. According to Freud's theory of humor and the relevant research, what do you expect to find in terms of the content of these nine jokes? After collecting the data, can you say that your expectation was confirmed? Speculate on the outcome of your study. (85-88)

5. State three specific predictions of Freud's theory about hostile humor. Summarize the evidence for a preference for hostile humor, the reduction of aggression with hostile humor, and the relationship between tension reduction and funniness. Give an alternative explanation for each of these predictions. (87-88)

6. Describe the continuum on which theorists fall with respect to hypnosis. What are the extreme positions on the continuum? Where do you fall on the continuum and why? (91)

7. According to socio-cognitive theories of hypnosis, what is the difference between hypnotized and nonhypnotized people who comply to a request? What criticisms have been made of the hidden observer demonstrations? Why have some argued that the psychoanalytic position on hypnosis is circular? (92-93)

8. List the techniques used to breach posthypnotic amnesia. List the methods that have been shown to increase hypnotic responsiveness. Explain why hypnosis is largely a participant variable. (93-94)

9. Is it possible to train people to be more responsive to hypnotic suggestions? Give an example of a study that demonstrated the researcher's ability to increase responsiveness. (94-96)

Evaluative Questions

1. Consider an example from your own life of a feeling or behavior that is readily explained by psychoanalytic theory. Specifically describe the insight psychoanalysis provides in this respect. Contrast the readily explained feeling or behavior with another that is not easily explained by psychoanalytic theory. (71-72)

2. Document a dream of your own that you remember from either the recent past or from childhood. Identify the symbols in the dream and give at least three different interpretations of your dream. Which interpretation appeals to you the most and why? (72-76)

3. Summarize the research findings that challenge Freud's theory of dreaming. Given that human adults are not the only creatures that experience REM sleep, evaluate the claim made by Freud that dreams are wish fulfillments of the unconscious. (77)

4. Given that Freud's approach to personality posits such a significant role for the unconscious in every aspect of our lives and its strong influence on our behaviors, what do you make of the various alternative explanations for unconscious influences on our behavior? Should we not find conclusive evidence for the existence of the unconscious and large effects of its influence on behavior? (79-80)

5. Describe the debate between the neodissociation view and the socio-cognitive view of hypnosis. Include the central issues and the explanations of hypnosis given by each of these approaches. With which do you agree and why? (92)

6. Describe the personality of an individual who is highly responsive to hypnosis. What are the characteristics of the hypnotically responsive person? Give examples from your own life to illustrate whether you possess the characteristics of a person who is responsive to hypnosis. (95-96)

Answers to Multiple Choice Questions

1.	a, 71	12.	d, 81
2.	b, 72	13.	b, 85
3.	c, 73	14.	b, 85
4.	c, 76	15.	d, 88
5.	d, 76	16.	a, 92
6.	d, 77	17.	b, 93
7.	c, 77	18.	d, 94
8.	c, 77	19.	c, 94
9.	c, 79	20.	d, 95
10.	a, 83	21.	c, 96
11.	c, 80		

Chapter 5

The Psychoanalytic Approach

Neo-Freudian Theory, Application, and Assessment

Limits and Liabilities of Freudian Theory

Alfred Adler

Carl Jung

Erik Erikson

Karen Horney

Harry Stack Sullivan

Erich Fromm

Application: Psychoanalytic Theory and Religion

Assessment: Measuring Types

Strengths and Criticisms of Neo-Freudian Theories

Learning Objectives

1. State three limits of Freudian theory. State the liabilities associated with each of these limitations.
2. Briefly sketch the life of Alfred Adler and describe his relationship to Freud. State how Adler's life experiences may have influenced his theory.
3. Discuss Adler's contribution to psychoanalytic theory and identify the main points of his approach. State the role of inferiority, birth order, and other basic factors that influence personality development in Adler's view.

4. Briefly sketch the life of Carl Jung and describe his relationship to Freud. State how Jung's life experiences may have influenced his theory.

5. Discuss Jung's contribution to psychoanalytic theory and identify the main points of his approach. Define collective unconscious and describe its contents. State the evidence Jung gave for the collective unconscious.

6. Briefly sketch the life of Erik Erikson and describe his relationship to Freud. State how Erikson's life experiences may have influenced his theory.

7. Discuss Erikson's contribution to psychoanalytic theory and identify the main points of his approach. Define identity crisis and describe Erikson's conception of the ego.

8. List the basic stages of personality development throughout the life cycle according to Erikson's theory. With each stage give an example of the basic crisis involved.

9. Briefly sketch the life of Karen Horney and describe her relationship to Freud. State how Horney's life experiences may have influenced her theory.

10. Discuss Horney's contribution to psychoanalytic theory and identify the specific objections she had to Freud's original theory. Explain Horney's conception of neurosis and discuss three general social interaction styles that neurotic people adopt.

11. Briefly sketch the life of Harry Stack Sullivan and describe his relationship to Freud. State how Sullivan's life experiences may have influenced his theory.

12. Discuss Sullivan's training and contribution to psychoanalytic theory. Define personifications and describe the role of social interactions in his approach.

13. List the developmental epochs according to Sullivan's theory and for each give a characterization of the epoch.

14. Briefly sketch the life of Erich Fromm and describe his relationship to Freud. State how Fromm's life experiences may have influenced his theory.

15. Discuss Fromm's contribution to psychoanalytic theory and specify the logic behind his approach. Describe three strategies people use to escape freedom and the concept of positive freedom according to Fromm.

16. State Freud's view of religion and its role in human life. Contrast Freud's view with that of Jung and Fromm. State Jung's answer to the question of God's existence. Also give Fromm's distinction between types of religions.

17. Compare the methods of assessment used by neo-Freudian psychologists to those used by Freud himself. Fully describe Jung's theory of psychological types and how it evolved.

18. Describe the Myers-Briggs Type Indicator and specify the contexts under which it is used for personality assessment. Explain the best ways in which the Myers-Briggs Type Indicator can be applied to education.

19. Discuss the strengths of the neo-Freudian theories of personality. Identify whether neo-Freudian approaches influenced later personality theorists.

20. Discuss two general criticisms that can be made of neo-Freudian theories of personality.

Important Concepts

neo-Freudians (p. 100)
striving for superiority (p. 102)
inferiority complex (p. 103)
analytic psychology (p. 106)
primordial images (p. 106)
personal unconscious (p. 106)
collective unconscious (p. 106)
anima (p. 107)
animus (p. 107)
shadow (p. 109)
identity crisis (p. 112)
neurosis (p. 117)
penis envy (p. 120)
womb envy (p. 120)
moving toward people (p. 119)
moving against people (p. 120)
moving away from people (p. 120)
feminine psychology (p. 120)
personifications (p. 122)
developmental epochs (p. 123)
authoritarianism (p. 125)
automaton conformity (p. 127)
positive freedom (p. 128)
humanistic religions (p. 130)
authoritarian religions (p. 130)
psychological types (p. 131)
extraversion (p. 131)
Myers-Briggs Type Indicator (p. 132)

InfoTrac *Search terms:*

Alfred Adler (p. 101)
individual psychology (p. 101)
birth order (p. 104)
Carl Jung (p. 106)
archetypes (p. 106)
Erik Erikson (p. 110)
ego psychology (p. 111)
Karen Horney (p. 117)
Erich Fromm (p. 125)
introversion (p. 131)

Programmed Review

In the early days of psychoanalysis, a failure to adhere strictly to Freud's theory was considered _________ .

blasphemy — p. 100

A child who is having feelings of inferiority is beginning a life long struggle, according to _________ .

Alfred Adler — p. 102

Adler's assessment of ________ children was positive.

middle p. 104

The neo-Freudian theorist who named his approach analytic psychology was ________ .

Carl Jung p. 106

Carl Jung believed we all have a part of our mind that Freud neglected to talk about called the ________ .

collective unconscious p. 106

The unconscious part of ourselves that is symbolized in the devil is known as ________ .

the shadow p. 109

The approach to personality developed by Erik Erikson is known as ________ .

ego psychology p. 111

Erik Erikson observed that overly protective parents hinder the development of a sense of what he called ________ .

autonomy p. 113

Within ego psychology the crisis faced by most young adults is ________ .

intimacy vs. isolation p. 114

Karen Horney said that __________ behavior starts with disturbed interpersonal relationships during childhood.

neurotic p. 117

People who tune out the world use a strategy for dealing with anxiety called moving __________ people.

away from p. 120

Harry Stack Sullivan's view of personality was that it does not even exist in the absence of _____________ .

interpersonal relations p. 121

The personification that reflects those parts of our experiences that we would rather not think about was called the __________ by Sullivan.

bad-me p. 123

The __________ is characterized by the need to have a same-sex "chum."

preadolescence epoch p. 124

Erich Fromm suggested that people who show a combination of striving for submission and for domination are using the method of escape called __________ .

authoritarianism p. 125

According to Fromm, humanistic religions are different from authoritarian religions in that they provide an opportunity for __________ .

personal growth p. 130

From careful observations Jung noted that sensation and feeling are the __________ functions because they are concerned with perception rather than reason.

irrational p. 131

An optimal setting for the __________ personality type is highly structured and organized.

judging p. 133

Multiple Choice Questions

1. Many theorists after Freud addressed the positive features of the ego and emphasized the role of __________ rather than unconscious determinants of behavior only.

    a. social and cultural influences
    b. adolescent and early adulthood experiences
    c. penis envy
    d. both a and b

2. Which of the following is *not* a key limitation to Freud's theory?

   a. the idea that the adult personality is formed by the time a child is five or six
   b. the idea that the ego defends against anxiety
   c. Freud's emphasis on instinctual influences on personality
   d. Freud's concentration on the negative parts of personality

3. Alfred Adler called his approach to personality

   a. individual psychology.
   b. ego psychology.
   c. feminine psychology.
   d. authoritarian psychology.

4. Rather than equate achievement with mental health, Adler argued that well-adjusted people strive for superiority through concern for

   a. younger generations.
   b. self-interest.
   c. social interest.
   d. personifications.

5. Who was the first neo-Freudian theorist to break with Freud?

   a. Carl Jung
   b. Karen Horney
   c. Erik Erikson
   d. Alfred Adler

6. According to Adler, two types of parental behavior that are sure to lead to personality problems are pampering and

   a. the birth of more children.
   b. neglect.
   c. overprotection.
   d. authoritarianism.

7. According to Adler, which of the following birth orders has the least number of personality problems?

   a. first-borns
   b. middle-borns
   c. last-borns
   d. only children

8. The __________ is made up of primordial images (archetypes).

   a. psychotic episode
   b. collective unconscious
   c. superego
   d. adult personality

9. Which of the following is a true statement about the collective unconscious?

   a. The collective unconscious consists of thoughts repressed out of consciousness.
   b. We acquire the collective unconscious from interactions with our parents.
   c. The collective unconscious is basically the same for all people.
   d. both a and c

10. Carl Jung's evidence for the collective unconscious consisted of

   a. an in-depth examination of the concept of ego.
   b. data from laboratory experiments and case studies.
   c. interpretation of Freud's central writings.
   d. folklore, art, mythology, and psychosis.

11. According to Erikson, adults who fail to develop concern for the development of young people suffer from a sense of

   a. relief.
   b. despair.
   c. stagnation.
   d. disaster.

12. Freud's anal stage of development is roughly related to which of Erikson's stages?

   a. trust vs. mistrust
   b. autonomy vs. shame and doubt
   c. initiative vs. guilt
   d. industry vs. inferiority

13. Jenny likes to play games with her friends and organize activities for her playmates. She is developing a sense of initiative through setting and achieving goals. According to Erikson, where in the life cycle is Jenny?

   a. young adulthood
   b. toddler
   c. early childhood
   d. adolescence

14. According to Erikson, a person in middle adulthood is most likely to be dealing with which of the following issues?

    a. whether or not to take an active role in the lives of young people
    b. whether or not to commit to a romantic relationship
    c. whether or not to feel guilty about facing challenges
    d. whether or not to feel satisfaction with choices made in life

15. Which term did Erikson use to describe the optimal outcome at the end of childhood?

    a. integrity
    b. initiative
    c. industry
    d. identity

16. One of the most important contributions to personality theory by Karen Horney was her view that neurotics are

    a. trapped in a self-defeating way of interacting with others.
    b. insecure about their dreams.
    c. really as healthy as any other individual.
    d. people who suffer from "womb envy."

17. Samantha is anxious about socializing with others and she acts so funny toward her peers when they invite her to go out with them that they have stopped asking. Which interaction style does Samantha display, according to Horney?

    a. moving toward people
    b. moving away from people
    c. moving against people
    d. moving without people

18. By introducing the concept of "womb envy," Horney was suggesting that

    a. men are as dissatisfied with themselves as women.
    b. men are conflicted as children over wanting a womb like mother has.
    c. women are ultimately superior to men because they can bear children.
    d. each gender has attributes that the other admires.

19. According to Sullivan, one effective way to reduce the impact of anxiety-provoking information is to use

    a. dream interpretation.
    b. womb envy.
    c. selective inattention.
    d. neurotic strategies.

20. George is thinking about the A grade he received on his psychology exam and how his studying increased his grade from his usual performance. Sullivan would say that George's personification is the

    a. not-me.
    b. bad-me.
    c. good-me.
    d. silly-me.

21. When we inevitably face a sense of insignificance about oneself, that we cannot control everything, Fromm suggested that we can choose to either escape freedom or

    a. progress to positive freedom.
    b. learn helplessness.
    c. embrace powerlessness.
    d. fail to take responsibility.

22. Jack works hard at his job and has achieved a level of security in his work and lifestyle by following the rules and fitting in. Erich Fromm would say that Jack has fulfilled his basic need to escape from the anxiety of freedom by

    a. becoming authoritarian.
    b. destroying all of life's threatening situations.
    c. automaton conformity.
    d. individuation.

23. The neo-Freudian theorist who stimulated the most discussion about religion was

    a. Alfred Alder.
    b. Carl Jung.
    c. Karen Horney.
    d. Erich Fromm.

24. Which of the following statements can be attributed to Jung's view of religion?

    a. "Authoritarian religions emphasize that we are controlled by a powerful God."
    b. "Modern psychotherapy has taken on the role once reserved for the clergy."
    c. "Humanistic religions emphasize that there is no God."
    d. "The religions of mankind must be classes among the mass-delusions."

25. Jung's theory of psychological types suggests that people who have an attitude of __________ have a dominant tendency to channel psychic energy inward.

    a. intuition
    b. inspiration
    c. extraversion
    d. introversion

26. At an art museum Julie considers the value of one work of art and says that the artist must have been depressed when he created it. Which of the following is most likely the dominant function for Julie?

    a. thinking
    b. intuition
    c. sensation
    d. feeling

27. In addition to the psychological types described by Jung, the Myers-Briggs Type Indicator measures

    a. whether one is open to new information.
    b. the sensing-intuitive categories.
    c. one's level of neurosis.
    d. both a and b

28. Like Freud's original theory, the neo-Freudian approach can be criticized for

    a. a lack of scientific evidence.
    b. being more descriptive than scientific.
    c. incomplete or limited accounts of personality.
    d. all of the above

Integrative Questions

1. List and elaborate on the three general limits and liabilities to Freud's theory. From your reading of the chapter, give specific examples of how neo-Freudian theorists handled these problems with Freud's theory. (101)

2. In what ways is the inferiority complex like the behavioral/learning approach's concept of learned helplessness? What is the motivating force in life, according to Adler? Does Alder's view suggest that mental health comes from achievement? Why or why not? (102-103)

3. Discuss the influence of parenting style and birth order on the personality according to Adler. Give examples of adult personalities that result from the three birth order categories. Identify yourself in terms of birth order and evaluate Adler's approach from your personal introspection. (103-105)

4. Describe each of the various archetypes proposed by Jung to be in the collective unconscious. In what ways is each reflected in our personalities and culture? What did Jung call the process of becoming what we're supposed to become? (107-109)

5. Contrast Erikson's conception of the ego with Freud's. In what specific ways does Erikson depart from Freud with respect to the ego and personality development? (110-112)

6. List each of the stages of development according to Erikson, including an example of each crisis. Contrast Erikson's stages of development with Sullivan's developmental epochs. In what ways do these schemes overlap? What characteristics and ages of onset are different between these two approaches? (112-116, 124)

7. Define "womb envy." Explain the reasoning behind this idea. (120)

8. Make a list of the names of the neo-Freudian theorists. Next to each name on the list write one fact that distinguishes the theorist or theory from all the others. (101-130)

9. What were the major influences on Fromm that led to his psychoanalytic theory? Discuss his mechanisms of escape and illustrate each with your own example. What defense mechanisms would Freud say roughly match each of Fromm's strategies? Explain. (125-127)

10. According to Fromm, what is the foremost component of spontaneity? Discuss a way in which Fromm's approach is similar to that of humanistic psychologists. (127)

11. What was Jung's main interest in religion? How did Jung answer the question of God's existence? Why, according to Jung, is there a similar entity to the Judeo-Christian God in all cultures of the world? (128-129)

12. In what ways is the Myers-Briggs Type Indicator similar to other personality assessment techniques? How might the Freudian defense mechanisms come into play during the testing of a personality using the Myers-Briggs Type Indicator? (133)

Evaluative Questions

1. Consider the manner in which Freud and those who disagreed with Freud were viewed by his admirers. Critically evaluate the scientific status of the contributions of the neo-Freudians who broke with Freud and elaborated his theory. (101, 135)

2. What are the differences between the instincts Freud proposed and what Jung meant by the collective unconscious? Did Jung think there was any difference? (106)

3. What is the main difficulty of Jungian psychology? What evidence did Jung provide for the collective unconscious? Based on the standards of scientific research you learned about in Chapter 2, state to what degree you think Jung's evidence was scientific. (109-110)

4. Consider each of the three strategies Horney proposed by which people handle anxiety. Think of someone you know for each of these strategies and give evidence to support your categorization of each person. (119-120)

5. What was Horney's explanation for Freud's observations and theories about women? What fundamental aspect of her approach is underscored by her difference with Freud over feminine psychology? (120-121)

6. Choose three neo-Freudian theorists and give a critical evaluation of each one's theory in three paragraphs. Then in the fourth paragraph give evidence for or against the validity of each theorist's approach in your life. (101-130)

7. Categorize yourself according to the eight psychological types in Table 5.2 on page 132 of your text. Now examine Table 5.3. Identify the kind of career that would be appropriate for your psychological type. Do the same for a friend and see if they agree with your analysis. (132-133)

Answers to Multiple Choice Questions

1.	d, 101	15.	c, 113
2.	b, 101	16.	a, 118
3.	a, 101	17.	b, 120
4.	c, 103	18.	d, 120
5.	d, 101	19.	c, 122
6.	b, 104	20.	c, 123
7.	b, 104	21.	a, 125
8.	b, 106	22.	c, 127
9.	c, 106	23.	b, 128
10.	d, 109	24.	b, 130
11.	c, 114	25.	d, 131
12.	b, 113	26.	d, 132
13.	c, 113	27.	a, 133
14.	a, 116	28.	d, 135

Chapter 6

The Neo-Freudian Theories

Relevant Research

Anxiety and Coping Strategies

Psychoanalytic Concepts and Aggression

Attachment Style and Adult Relationships

Learning Objectives

1. Give evidence to support the claim that we live in an age of anxiety.
2. Identify three types of anxiety according to Freud. State the purpose of coping strategies as seen by neo-Freudian theorists and what some neo-Freudians meant by "defense mechanisms."
3. Distinguish coping strategies that are active from those that are avoidant and distinguish coping strategies that are problem-focused from emotion-focused strategies. State the relative effectiveness of these different strategies.
4. State the ideas behind Freud's frustration-aggression hypothesis. Discuss three psychoanalytic concepts that aggression researchers have adopted.
5. Summarize the research findings from tests of the frustration-aggression hypothesis. Give evidence that frustration is one cause of aggression. Elaborate on the newer way of looking at frustration and aggression by listing advantages of the newer version.
6. Describe how one displaces aggression and when displacement is most likely to occur.
7. Define catharsis and give its role in aggressive behavior. Give the research evidence that supports the original frustration-aggression hypothesis and evidence that aggression does not lead to reduced aggression.

8. Explain why understanding adult romantic relationships begins with looking at very early childhood experiences. Discuss object relations theory and attachment theory and their essential concepts. Specify three types of parent-child relationships and give an example of each.
9. Describe three major adult attachment styles and the alternative four-category model of attachment styles based on the dimensions of avoidance and dependence. Give the major contrasting feature between these models.
10. State how adult attachment styles relate to happiness in romantic relationships. Provide examples of the kinds of interactions partners have within each of the major attachment styles.

Important Concepts

reality anxiety (p. 139)
neurotic anxiety (p. 139)
moral anxiety (p. 139)
repressors (p. 142)
sensitizers (p. 142)
active-cognitive strategies (p. 143)
active-behavioral strategies (p. 143)
avoidance strategies (p. 144)
problem-focused strategies (p. 144)
emotion-focused strategies (p. 144)
coping flexibility (p. 146)
Thanatos (p. 147)
frustration-aggression hypothesis (p. 147)
catharsis (p. 148)
sublimation (p. 148)
displacement (p. 151)
object relations theory (p. 156)
attachment (p. 156)
attachment theory (p. 156)
avoidant style (p. 157)
secure attachment style (p. 157)
anxious-ambivalent style (p. 157)
four-category model (p. 159)
disoriented/fearful style (p. 160)

InfoTrac *Search terms:*

anxiety (p. 139)
coping strategies (p. 140)
coping style (p. 141)
aggression (p. 147)
attachment relationships (p. 156)

Programmed Review

When you experience _________, you have feelings of worry, panic, and fear.

anxiety p. 139

Karen Horney agreed with Freud that _________ conflicts often trigger anxiety.

unconscious p. 140

People who actively think about a stressful situation to try to make things better use the __________ coping strategy.

active-cognitive p. 142

In general, active coping strategies are __________ effective in helping people with a wide variety of stressors than avoidance strategies.

more p. 145

Some investigators have found that problem-focused coping strategies are more effective than emotion-focused strategies in helping __________ in social relationships.

soldiers p. 146

Freud suggested that when the libido is frustrated we experience a __________ of aggressing against the obstacle.

primordial reaction p. 147

The newer view of aggression argues that frustrations cause us to act aggressively because they are __________ .

unpleasant p. 150

One explanation for why aggression leads to more aggression is that it is __________ by the cathartic release of tension.

reinforced p. 155

Emotional attachment between infants and their caregivers is often called __________ .

attachment relationships p. 156

A person who describes their relationships with family members as distrustful and emotionally distant most probably has __________ style of attachment.

an avoidant p. 157

In terms of the four-category model of adult attachment, __________ people have feelings that they are unworthy while they tend to see others as trustworthy.

preoccupied p. 160

In a longitudinal study, a team of investigators showed that __________ adults had a long history of stable and satisfying romantic relationships.

secure p. 161

Multiple Choice Questions

1. In the last decades, several studies on the relationship between frustration and aggression have
   a. taken researchers far from psychoanalytic roots.
   b. given strong support to Freudian concepts.
   c. demonstrated that the neo-Freudian theories do not give a clear account when it comes to aggression.
   d. found little support for a connection.

2. Harold feels anxious whenever the cheerleaders at school walk close by. Whenever some girls speak to him, Harold turns red and often cannot speak. Which form of anxiety is Harold most likely experiencing?
   a. reality anxiety
   b. neurotic anxiety
   c. moral anxiety
   d. superego anxiety

3. In one study when participants were shown a film on industrial safety, the most common strategy for reducing the anxiety produced by the film was to
   a. focus on technical aspects of the film rather than the discomfort of the content.
   b. close their eyes or look away.
   c. remind themselves that what they were watching was only a film.
   d. make jokes about the more grisly scenes.

4. Jorge is facing a very difficult midterm exam and is feeling anxiety about it. As the exam date approaches and his anxiety increases, Jorge starts thinking about ways to study more effectively and schedules a large portion of time for active study of the material on the test. In terms of coping, which of the following is Jorge's strategy?
   a. avoidance strategy
   b. repression strategy
   c. emotion-focused strategy
   d. problem-focused strategy

5. Because researchers have been able to identify stable patterns in the way people deal with anxiety, psychologists often refer to a person's general approach to coping as

   a. one's coping style.
   b. a self-fulfilling prophecy.
   c. one's cathartic style.
   d. coping solutions.

6. Along the repression-sensitization dimension, repressors

   a. try to think about a threatening situation in a rational way.
   b. try to avoid threatening situations.
   c. find out as much as possible about the stressful situation.
   d. use active-cognitive coping strategies.

7. With respect to gender differences in coping strategies,

   a. women use emotion-focused strategies more than men.
   b. men use emotion-focused strategies more than women.
   c. women take steps to solve problems directly more than men.
   d. none of the above

8. Which of the following is true about the effectiveness of coping strategies?

   a. The more people rely on coping strategies, the more anxiety they feel.
   b. Active strategies are more effective than avoidant strategies.
   c. The use of a coping strategy is more effective in reducing anxiety than not using one.
   d. Avoidance strategies are generally more effective in the long run.

9. When investigators examined the coping strategies of Israeli soldiers who had suffered combat stress, which of the following was found to be most successful?

   a. emotion-focused strategies
   b. problem-focused strategies
   c. either problem-focused or emotion-focused strategies
   d. only avoidant strategies

10. Because different coping strategies work under different situations, researchers often call the ability to know when to apply which strategy

   a. coping-effective pattern.
   b. anxiety reduction style.
   c. coping flexibility.
   d. none of the above

11. Which of the following is the name Freud gave to the death instinct?

    a. the Shadow
    b. libido
    c. Thanatos
    d. catharsis

12. With regard to the frustration-aggression hypothesis,

    a. most researchers today accept that aggression is always caused by frustration.
    b. it has been shown that aggression is always reduced by catharsis.
    c. frustration always leads to aggressive behavior.
    d. most researchers today accept that aggression can have a number of causes.

13. To explain why and when aggression will decrease, many researchers have adopted the Freudian concept of

    a. the Oedipus complex.
    b. repression.
    c. the superego.
    d. catharsis.

14. Which of the following is true about the frustration-aggression hypothesis?

    a. Frustrated people act more aggressively than nonfrustrated people.
    b. Frustration is one cause of aggression.
    c. Aggressive responses are more likely when a frustrated person is close to their goal.
    d. all of the above

15. When angry participants in a study were allowed to retaliate against someone who frustrated them,

    a. the participants' blood pressure went up.
    b. greater aggression was shown after the participants experienced a release of tension.
    c. greater aggression was shown when there was no opportunity for cathartic release.
    d. acting aggressively led to inhibition of further aggression.

16. In contrast to Freud's theory, object relations theorists

    a. focus on internal drives and conflicts.
    b. are interested in the intellectual and emotional development of the infant.
    c. do not believe that children develop unconscious representations of significant objects in their environment.
    d. are interested in an infant's relationship with his or her parents.

17. Which of the following statements would most likely be said by a person with an anxious-ambivalent style?

    a. "I'm uncomfortable around other people."
    b. "It is easy for me to get close to people."
    c. "I'm worried that my partner doesn't really love me."
    d. "Lovers often want to get more intimate with me than I want."

18. In a newspaper survey, secure adults reported that they had been in their current relationship

    a. for more than ten years.
    b. for less than six years.
    c. since puberty.
    d. for more than thirty years.

19. Sarah is a single, twenty-eight-year-old woman. She feels pressure from her family to get married and have a family of her own, but she is very reluctant to trust the men she meets. Sarah's attachment style can be classified as

    a. secure.
    b. preoccupied.
    c. dismissing.
    d. disoriented.

20. Which of the following categories of adult attachment is best characterized by fears of abandonment?

    a. avoidant
    b. dismissing
    c. anxious
    d. fearful

Integrative Questions

1. Contrast the strategies proposed by the neo-Freudian theorists that people use to reduce anxiety with the defense mechanisms Freud proposed. What is the essential difference between Freudian and neo-Freudian perspectives? (141-144)

2. State the early version of the distinction between active and avoidant coping strategies. Give some examples of a person's response to stress from each end of the dimension. (141-144)

3. Which are the most effective coping strategies for reducing anxiety? From the evidence given in your textbook, give your best answer and support it. (144-146)

4. Given what you know about the neo-Freudian approaches of Horney and Fromm, how would each of these theorists explain aggressive behavior and what role would frustration play in their views? (117, 125, 148)

5. Discuss how Freud's original frustration-aggression hypothesis influenced research by behavioral psychologists on the topic. In what ways do the Freudian and behavioral approaches differ with respect to frustration-aggression? In what way is the revised frustration-aggression hypothesis even more behavioral in approach? (147-151, 420)

6. Describe three kinds of parent-child attachment relationships. What are the implications for children in each of these relationships when they are adults? What will their romantic relationships probably be like? (156-159, 160-163)

7. Contrast with examples each of the four categories of attachment styles in the alternate model of adult attachment styles. What would an adult's attachment style be like who has a negative model of self and a positive model of others? What about a person who has a positive model of self and a negative model of others? (159-163)

Evaluative Questions

1. From the list of coping strategies in Table 6.1 of your text, choose three coping strategies you have used recently and critically evaluate how effective each one was for reducing your anxiety. From your own experience, which type of strategy appears most effective? (143-146)

2. Choose two examples of research from the chapter and identify the psychoanalytic concepts involved in the research. How did the neo-Freudians adapt each concept from Freud's original formulation? How do you suppose Freud would object to each adaptation? (140, 148, 156)

3. Consider avoidance strategies as a means of reducing anxiety. Describe two situations in which avoidance would be an effective coping strategy. (144)

4. Summarize the findings of the research on aggression using electric shock. How was catharsis measured in this study and what evidence was given for the frustration-aggression hypothesis? Speculate about the ethical dilemmas posed by the method of this research and potential rival hypotheses for the results. (153-155)

5. Specify the improvements of the four-category model of attachment styles over the three-category model. If you believe there are none, state why not. Does the four category model include all the possible styles of adult attachment? Support your answer with examples of people you know or relationships you've been in. (156-160)

6. From the specific connections between early childhood attachments and adult attachment styles in intimate relationships, speculate on the account of these connections that Erik Erikson would give. What would be the greatest contributing factor to anxious and preoccupied styles according to Erikson? to avoidant and dismissing styles? Give one means of reconciling Erikson's neo-Freudian approach with attachment theory. (114, 156-159)

Answers to Multiple Choice Questions

1. a, 138
2. b, 139
3. c, 140
4. d, 144
5. a, 141
6. b, 142
7. a, 144
8. c, 145
9. b, 146
10. c, 146
11. c, 147
12. d, 150
13. d, 152
14. d, 153
15. b, 154
16. d, 156
17. c, 157
18. a, 158
19. c, 159
20. d, 160

Answers to Multiple Choice Questions

Chapter 7

The Trait Approach

Theory, Application, and Assessment

The Trait Approach

Important Trait Theorists

Factor Analysis and the Search for the Structure of Personality

The Situation versus Trait Controversy

Application: The Big Five in the Workplace

Assessment: Self-Report Inventories

Strengths and Criticisms of the Trait Approach

Learning Objectives

1. Discuss the reasons why personality researchers today do not use a strict type approach to personality.
2. State the characteristics of the trait approach to personality. Distinguish the special features of the trait approach from other approaches to personality, including one major advantage of studying personality through the trait approach.
3. Discuss the contributions of Gordon Allport to understanding personality and explain why his work was "groundbreaking." Distinguish between nomothetic and idiographic approaches and the three kinds of personality traits proposed by Allport.
4. Define and discuss the terms functional autonomy and proprium. Explain how Allport's approach differs from the psychoanalytic approach with respect to childhood experiences in particular.
5. Discuss the contributions of Henry Murray to understanding personality. Give the name of Murray's approach and discuss the kinds of needs he considered central to personality. Define the concept known as press and state Murray's legacy.

6. State the central goal of Raymond Cattell in the trait approach to personality and how his work differed from that of Allport and Murray. Discuss your understanding of the technique of factor analysis.
7. Explain how the traits that make up personality are organized into a structure. List and define the factors identified by researchers as the Big Five. Discuss some criticisms and limitations of the Big Five Model of personality structure.
8. Summarize the situation versus trait controversy. Discuss two criticisms of the trait approach given by Mischel with respect to this controversy. Give a defense of the trait approach and specify how the criticisms and defense have improved our understanding of personality traits.
9. Discuss how the Big Five Model is applied in the workplace. State the relative desirability of different personality characteristics for job performance.
10. Explain why self-report inventories are so popular in professional psychology. Describe the Minnesota Multiphasic Personality Inventory and state what psychologists look for in the resulting scores.
11. List three problems associated with self-report inventories and give an example of each problem. State specific defenses against these problems and ways to address them when collecting data.
12. Identify three strengths of the trait approach to personality. State why the trait approach is an important theoretical perspective. State the general criticisms that have been made of the trait approach.

Important Concepts

trait (p. 166)
common traits (p. 169)
central traits (p. 169)
nomothetic approach (p. 169)
idiographic approach (p. 169)
cardinal traits (p. 169)
secondary traits (p. 171)
functional autonomy (p. 171)
personology (p. 173)
need for Achievement (p.173)
need for Affiliation (p. 173)
viscerogenic need (p. 173)
proprium (p. 173)
psychogenic need (p. 173)
press (p. 173)
factor analysis (p. 175)
source traits (p. 177)
the Big Five (p. 177)
openness (p. 180)
conscientiousness (p. 180)
cross-situational consistency (p. 185)
person-by-situation approach (p. 185)
aggregate data (p. 187)
acquiescence response (p. 199)

InfoTrac *Search terms:*

trait (p. 166)
extraversion (p. 179)
neuroticism (p. 179)
Minnesota Multiphasic Personality Inventory (p. 192)
agreeableness (p. 180)
social desirability (p. 197)

Programmed Review

The first attempt to identify and describe the structural characteristics of personality was to develop ________ systems.

typology p. 165

Trait psychologists believe that one can take any person and place him or her somewhere along a ________ .

continuum p. 165

Trait psychologists differ from other approaches because they are usually less interested in ________ one's behavior in a given situation.

predicting p. 166

Trait psychologists are more likely to be ________ than practicing therapists.

academic researchers p. 168

The nomothetic approach to personality measurement looks at _______ traits.

common p. 169

Allport argued that there is no reason to assume the adult behavior stems from the same motives as earlier behavior because in adulthood behavior has become ________ .

functionally autonomous p. 171

The ________ is a term used to describe all aspects of the self united under a single concept.

proprium p. 173

According to Murray, each of us can be described in terms of a personal ________ .

hierarchy of needs p. 173

The projective test developed by Murray is the ________ .

Thematic Apperception Test (TAT) p. 174

Raymond Cattell argued that psychologists should not begin with a ________ list of personality traits.

preconceived p. 175

To discover the structure of personality, Cattell used a sophisticated statistical technique called ________ .

factor analysis p. 175

The ________ dimension of the Big Five categorizes people according to their level of emotional stability and personal adjustment.

neuroticism p. 179

When ________ terms are included in the factor analysis of personality, two additional personality factors emerge in the new structure.

evaluative p. 182

Today most psychologists agree that the person and the situation ________ to determine behavior.

interact p. 185

A trait is more likely to predict a person's behavior if that trait is ________ for the person.

relevant or central p. 188

Research has shown that among the Big Five personality factors, the best predictor of performance is ________ .

conscientiousness p. 190

Employers have used scores from ________ to make hiring and promotion decisions for many years.

personality tests p. 190

________ are more widely used today than any other form of personality assessment.

Self-report inventories p. 192

Of particular interest to psychologists who use personality inventories are scores that are significantly ________ than those obtained by most test takers.

higher or lower p. 193

When people try to present themselves on a self-report inventory as better than they really are in order to get a job, then they are ________ good.

faking p. 193

The extent to which people present themselves in a favorable light is called ________ .

social desirability p. 197

Social desirability scores are useful when testing the ________ validity of a new personality scale or measure.

discriminant p. 199

Multiple Choice Questions

1. The type approach assumes that every person fits into one personality category and

   a. we can measure the instability of personality structure over time.
   b. these categories are represented along a continuum.
   c. the behavior of people in one category is different from people in another category.
   d. all people within a category can vary in the degree to which they fit it.

2. Which of the following is true about the trait approach?

   a. No major schools of psychotherapy have evolved from the trait approach.
   b. The trait approach is the best approach for predicting change in personality.
   c. Most trait researchers do not focus on predicting behavior.
   d. Trait theorists place the most emphasis on identifying the mechanisms that determine behavior.

3. Brad is a trait psychologist who works as a researcher at the local university. Brad attempts to identify behavior patterns that can be represented along a continuum. From his research he found that

   a. any person can be described by a list of discrete personality characteristics.
   b. not everyone's personality can be accurately measured.
   c. relatively few people score extremely high or low along a trait dimension.
   d. personality characteristics can change a great deal across situations.

4. The major trait theorists went beyond the examination of a few traits and

   a. described the nature of traits.
   b. explained the relationship between the traits and other psychological factors.
   c. described the structure of personality.
   d. all of the above

5. The trait approach is built on the assumption that personality characteristics are relatively stable over time and that

   a. personality characteristics are relatively stable over situations too.
   b. through trait descriptions we can make comparisons across people.
   c. the typical behavior of a person with one trait is different from that of another.
   d. while explanation is not possible, trait researchers focus on describing personality.

6. An advantage of using an idiographic approach to personality is that

   a. researchers can compare all people on measures of a certain trait.
   b. it reveals common traits.
   c. the person rather than the researcher determines what traits to examine.
   d. it provides information about the relationship between traits and behavior.

7. People with traits that dominate their personality can be described with a

   a. cardinal trait.
   b. central trait.
   c. idiographic map.
   d. secondary trait.

8. Sally appears to be a neat freak because her apartment is always clean and tidy and her belongings are well organized. Her neatness has become functionally autonomous. As a child, Sally probably

   a. kept her bedroom tidy in order to easily find all of her things.
   b. picked up her things in order to please her parents.
   c. sucked her thumb until she went to high school.
   d. had an imaginary friend that told her to be neat and organized.

9. Which of the following is *not* a psychogenic need?

   a. affiliation
   b. sexual intercourse
   c. autonomy
   d. safety

10. Henry Murray proposed that each person can be described by a personal hierarchy of needs that

   a. he used to adequately predict behavior.
   b. is used to compare one person's needs to other's.
   c. assists therapists in explaining one's behavior.
   d. none of the above

11. Murray referred to each environmental force that activates a need as a

   a. trigger.
   b. repressor.
   c. press.
   d. itch.

12. According to Cattell, _________ traits are traits that ultimately constitute the human personality.

   a. cardinal
   b. source
   c. secondary
   d. factor

13. Which of the following is *not* a factor among the Big Five?

   a. psychoticism
   b. neuroticism
   c. openness
   d. agreeableness

14. People high on the _________ dimension are helpful and sympathetic to others.

   a. agreeableness
   b. openness
   c. conscientiousness
   d. psychoticism

15. Steven is a college sophomore who likes to go to the weekly campus lecture series and take courses outside of his major. Given this information, trait researchers would classify Steven as high in

   a. neuroticism.
   b. agreeableness.
   c. openness.
   d. achievement.

16. Jimmy seems to be extremely disorganized with his books and papers, and his answers on homework are seldom presented in a clear and organized fashion. When called upon in class, Jimmy often needs the question repeated because of distractions. On which one of the Big Five dimensions of personality would Jimmy score low?

    a. agreeableness
    b. extraversion
    c. openness
    d. conscientiousness

17. Which of the following is true about the five-factor model?

    a. Few have criticized it for its lack of predictive value.
    b. Hypotheses about the origin of the five factors were generated after the results of the research were seen.
    c. Trait theorists would be better off focusing their research on the five main traits.
    d. both b and c

18. According to Walter Mischel, the trait approach to personality

    a. is the basis for decisions of little consequence to the person.
    b. does not predict behavior well.
    c. provides evidence of consistency of behaviors across situations.
    d. all of the above

19. Epstein has argued that the reason many researchers fail to produce strong links between personality traits and behavior is that

    a. they don't measure behavior correctly.
    b. they don't measure personality traits correctly.
    c. they don't perform the correct statistical analysis.
    d. none of the above

20. In psychological testing, a 100-item test has a greater __________ than a test with only two yes-no questions.

    a. validity
    b. internal consistency
    c. reliability
    d. significance

21. Which of the following is *not* a problem with self-report inventories?

    a. scoring
    b. carelessness
    c. faking
    d. response tendencies

22. Rosenthal, who compared the amount of variance accounted for in personality research to variance accounted for in other fields, found little evidence for a correlation between

    a. smoking and heart attack.
    b. taking aspirin and heart attack.
    c. alcohol abuse and heart attack.
    d. taking AZT and heart attack.

23. Rather than examine a large number of personality variables that may or may not be related to how well people perform in the workplace, many researchers now address the questions of personality and job performance

    a. by using the several psychogenic needs developed by Murray.
    b. by using the personality dimensions identified in the Big Five Model.
    c. by categorizing workers by personality types.
    d. by responses to work interests on self-report inventories.

24. Among the criticisms of the MMPI are questions about

    a. the validity of the scales.
    b. the appropriateness of some of the norm data.
    c. the nature of some of the constructs being measured.
    d. all of the above

25. Paul is a subject in personality research and fills out a lengthy personality inventory. While answering the questions, Paul begins to respond with answers that make him look better than if were answering completely honestly. Paul's response tendency is

    a. sabotaging the entire research study.
    b. known as carelessness.
    c. impossible to discover.
    d. known as social desirability.

26. In which way is the trait approach similar to other approaches to personality?

    a. Trait theorists tend to be academic researchers.
    b. Trait researchers rarely try to understand the behavior of just one person.
    c. Trait theory has generated a great deal of research.
    d. Trait theorists use objective measures to examine their constructs.

Integrative Questions

1. Discuss several ways in which the trait approach differs from other approaches to personality. Who is studied? What do trait theorists try to describe and predict? What do trait theorists have to say about personality change? (165-167)

2. List three fundamental ways in which Allport disagreed with Freud. What alternative explanations for adult behavior and personality did Allport propose? (168-171)

3. Following the description in the textbook, describe the general process of factor analysis. What is the result of such an analysis? What did Cattell discover concerning the structure of personality using this technique? (175, 177)

4. List and describe each of the personality dimensions known as the Big Five. How would you describe the popular comic strip character Charlie Brown in terms of the Big Five and why? (177-180)

5. How do modern personality psychologists answer the question of whether personality or situations determine behavior? Give the reasons why we can say there is little evidence for cross-situational consistency. Explain in your own words why personality researchers have failed to find a strong link between personality and behavior. (183-186)

6. Why are self-report inventories so popular as a means of assessing personality traits? Describe the differences between self-reports and other personality tests such as projective tests and behavioral observation. (61, 192-199, 400)

7. List and discuss the advantages of the trait approach to personality. What are the basic criticisms of this approach? Is it a problem that there is no single framework or theory of personality traits on which psychologists agree? Is the fact that the trait approach has not generated a school of psychotherapy a problem? Why or why not? (199-201)

Evaluative Questions

1. Gordon Allport said, "Psychologists would do well to give full recognition to manifest motives before probing the unconscious." State in a paragraph what you think Allport meant by this statement. Of Freud and Allport, who acknowledged the limitations of his theory? What were some of the limitations this theorist acknowledged? (168-169)

2. Describe yourself in terms of the hierarchy of needs proposed by Murray. Give an example from your own experience over the past two months of a press and how it worked with your needs to determine your behavior. (172-173)

3. Given the evidence in favor of the Big Five Model of personality, why would trait theorists not be better off examining only those five main traits? Give two criticisms of the Big Five Model and a response to these criticisms. What is your position on the Big Five Model? (181-183)

4. Where does your opinion fall in the person versus situation controversy? Do you think it is appropriate to make decisions about mental health or employment decisions based solely on personality test scores? Why or why not? (183-186)

5. Suppose you were measured along the Big Five traits for a new job. Give the best combination of traits from the perspective of the employer and compare it with the particular traits you think best represent you. (190-192)

Answers to Multiple Choice Questions

1. c, 165
2. a, 168
3. c, 166
4. d, 168
5. a, 166
6. c, 169
7. a, 169
8. b, 171
9. d, 173
10. d, 173
11. c, 173
12. b, 177
13. a, 179
14. a, 179
15. c, 180
16. d, 180
17. b, 182
18. b, 184
19. a, 186
20. b, 186
21. a, 193
22. b, 189
23. b, 190
24. d, 193
25. d, 197
26. c, 200

Chapter 8

The Trait Approach

Relevant Research

Achievement Motivation

Type A-Type B Behavior Patterns

Social Anxiety

Emotions

Optimism and Pessimism

Learning Objectives

1. Discuss what is meant by the trait called Achievement Motivation, listing the characteristics of people with high need for Achievement. Describe a common way psychologists measure Achievement Motivation.
2. State how need for Achievement can be predicted from what parents promote in the behavior of their children.
3. Explain how need for Achievement is related to both gender and culture. Specify how men and women differ in their definition of success.
4. Discuss attributions as a cognitive factor that influences achievement behavior. Describe three dimensions that determine the kind of attributions a person makes. Discuss the use of achievement goals in achievement situations. Give examples of four different kinds of achievement goals.
5. Define Type A and Type B behavior. List the many ways in which Type A people differ from Type B people. Discuss the relationship between Type A behavior as a personality variable and achievement.
6. Specify how Type A behavior can impact one's health. Discuss the problems of validity associated with measuring Type A and how identifying the toxic component of Type A is related to levels of anger and hostility.

7. Define social anxiety and distinguish it from other kinds of anxiety. List and discuss the characteristics of socially anxious people.
8. State how personality psychologists explain social anxiety. Discuss the reasons for shyness and evaluate the methods of reducing social anxiety.
9. Define and distinguish among three aspects of emotion that can be examined like personality traits. Describe the characteristics of each aspect of emotion in terms of predictable behavior patterns.
10. Define the personality variable dispositional optimism. Explain how optimism and pessimism are related to the way people face life's challenges by employing coping strategies. State the advantages of dispositional optimism for good health.
11. Define defensive pessimism and what motivates pessimistic personalities. State one way in which defensive pessimists differ from dispositional optimists with respect to coping strategies and anxiety level.

Important Concepts

need for Achievement (p. 204)
locus (p. 211)
control (p. 211)
stability (p. 211)
achievement goals (p. 212)
mastery goals (p. 212)
performance goals (p. 212)
valence (p. 213)
coronary-prone behavior pattern (p. 215)
toxic component (p. 219)
evaluation apprehension (p. 226)
emotional affectivity (p. 228)
positive affect (p. 228)
negative affect (p. 228)
affect intensity (p. 232)
emotional expressiveness (p. 234)
dispositional optimism (p. 236)
defensive pessimism (p. 240)

InfoTrac *Search terms*:

attributions (p. 211)
Type A personality (p. 215)
Type B personality (p. 215)
hostility (p. 219)
social anxiety (p. 223)

Programmed Review

For many psychologists personality research has become synonymous with the ___________ and examination of traits.

measurement p. 203

Predictably, high need achievers don't work hard at everything but tackle tasks with the potential for __________ with much energy.

personal achievement p. 206

Research suggests that too much parental involvement can stifle a child's sense of _________ .

independence p. 207

Presidents whose inaugural speeches indicated a high need for Achievement usually are rated by historians as __________ leaders.

ineffective p. 208

As career aspirations have changed over the past few decades, _________ have been more successful in the business world.

women p. 208

The meaning of __________ can vary as a function of culture.

achievement p. 209

An example of a cognitive personality variable that provides targets to which people aspire is called _________ .

achievement goals p. 212

Another name for the personality dimension known as Type A is _________ .

coronary-prone behavior pattern p. 215

Type A people often deal with arousal due to physiological stress by _________ .

denial p. 216

The most popular self-report measure of Type A personality is _________ .

the Jenkins Activity Survey p. 219

People high in __________ might become very upset when they are waiting in a slow-moving line.

hostility p. 219

Shy people are more likely than nonshy people to _________ .

blush p. 225

Most researchers today appear to use the terms social anxiety and __________ synonymously.

shyness p. 228

Researchers investigating social anxiety have consistently found that about _________ percent of the people surveyed identify themselves as shy.

40 p. 229

Shy persons' social interaction style is a type of __________ .

self-protective strategy p. 231

Researchers have used the __________ statistical technique to examine the relation among various emotions.

factor analysis p. 233

Affect intensity refers to the __________ to which people typically experience their emotions.

degree (strength) p. 238

Heart transplant patients with positive expectations do better __________ to life after surgery than those with a pessimistic outlook.

adjusting p. 242

Defensive pessimists generate their gloomy expectations as part of a deliberate __________ for dealing with upcoming events.

strategy p. 246

Multiple Choice Questions

1. Research on Type A behavior began as

   a. a study of individual differences in personality and later became useful in applied areas.
   b. an important means of understanding social anxiety.
   c. an applied concept and later came under the study of academic researchers.
   d. an example of a defense mechanism.

2. The original researchers of achievement motivation were not interested in all kinds of achievement. They specifically were interested in

   a. achievement in school.
   b. entrepreneurial behavior.
   c. individual differences in achievement behavior.
   d. cultural difference in achievement concepts.

3. The opportunity to receive clear __________ for their performance is important to persons high in need for Achievement.

   a. directions
   b. feedback
   c. rewards
   d. plans

4. Which of the following is indicative of high need for Achievement?

   a. a student who is motivated to avoid failure on an exam
   b. a businessperson who takes chances to get ahead
   c. a gambler who will only bet on a sure thing
   d. an employee who works hard at very boring tasks

5. Good advice for parents who want to raise their children to have high need for Achievement is to

   a. continue giving encouragement and support in every activity of the child.
   b. involve themselves in all of the child's interests.
   c. not give the child rewards for personal accomplishments.
   d. find a balance between encouragement and robbing the child of initiative.

6. Which of the following has been a fruitful division of achievement motivation in researchers' understanding of individual differences?

   a. desire to do a good job
   b. desire to compete with others
   c. desire to master difficult tasks
   d. all of the above

7. With respect to gender, nearly all of the early research in achievement motivation was conducted on

   a. males.
   b. females.
   c. high achievers.
   d. business executives.

8. Which of the following is true about gender and achievement?

   a. Women and men act similarly in achievement settings.
   b. Men and women differ in the way they define success.
   c. Women in our society are more likely to see success in terms of external standards.
   d. Men and women assign similar values to achievement tasks.

9. According to the ___________ approach to achievement motivation, we often ask ourselves why we have done as well as we have.

   a. achievement goals
   b. nomothetic
   c. factor analysis
   d. attribution

10. Which of the following is *not* a dimension of attributions?

   a. reliability
   b. stability
   c. locus
   d. control

11. In terms of specific achievement goals, mastery goals are

   a. characteristic of people with high need for Affiliation.
   b. related to one's desire to dominate or be master over others.
   c. concerned with developing competency in various tasks.
   d. none of the above

12. Jerry and George work for an advertising agency in Chicago. Jerry has been classified as Type A and George has been labeled Type B by their employer. Which of the following is a likely difference between Jerry and George?

   a. George works harder than Jerry but does not receive as much reward for his work.
   b. Jerry deals with frustrating situations with aggressiveness.
   c. George believes that time is important and shouldn't be wasted.
   d. Jerry does not procrastinate as often as George.

13. In a study of varying task difficulty, researchers have found that under threat to their perception of control,

    a. the most difficult task aroused Type B participants more than Type A.
    b. the most difficult task aroused Type A participants more than Type B.
    c. Type B participants were more aroused than Type A for all difficulty levels.
    d. arousal levels did not differ between easy and difficult tasks.

14. According to laboratory experiments that examine how Type A and Type B people respond to achievement tasks, the single best way to motivate a Type A person is

    a. by giving them plenty of time to perform a task.
    b. the opportunity to be challenged.
    c. by setting up a situation of competition.
    d. by making the task an easy one.

15. Most of the failure to uncover a significant relationship between Type A behavior and heart disease occurred when investigators used

    a. behavioral observation.
    b. self-report inventories.
    c. the Thematic Apperception Test.
    d. none of the above

16. Shy people often stumble over their words, say the wrong thing, and show outward signs of

    a. achievement motivation.
    b. clumsiness.
    c. wrongdoing.
    d. nervousness.

17. Which of the following statements is true about social anxiety?

    a. Socially anxious people recognize the source of their anxiety.
    b. Social anxiety can result from anticipated social interactions.
    c. We can identify a relatively stable tendency for people to experience social anxiety.
    d. all of the above

18. In a study in which participants were asked to engage in a five-minute "get acquainted" conversation, researchers found that

    a. socially anxious people were less likely to agree with the other person.
    b. little attempt was made by shy people to be polite to the other person.
    c. shy people attempt to minimize the amount of evaluation by the other person.
    d. all of the above

19. Lisa frequently experiences nervousness in her job and can become angry when the pressures of her work increase. Which dimension of emotion is illustrated by Lisa's behavior at work?

    a. positive affect
    b. negative affect
    c. intensity
    d. expressiveness

20. Which of the following has been demonstrated by research on emotional affectivity?

    a. Negative affect is related to psychological stress.
    b. People with positive affect report more health problems.
    c. Negative affect is related to social activity.
    d. all of the above

21. Emotional expressiveness refers to a person's __________ of emotions.

    a. strength
    b. memory
    c. inner conflict
    d. outward display

22. Which of the following is true about emotional expressiveness?

    a. The more expressive of emotions, the fewer problems in romantic relationships.
    b. Highly expressive people tend to have higher self-esteem.
    c. Women tend to be more expressive than men.
    d. all of the above

23. Research found that women going through surgery for breast cancer experienced less __________ during the year following surgery if they were optimistic rather than pessimistic individuals.

    a. recurrence
    b. family support
    c. distress
    d. fatigue

24. Which of the following is a reason why defensive pessimists deliberately take a pessimistic approach?

    a. to set themselves up for success
    b. to prepare themselves for failure
    c. to reduce the need to try harder
    d. to make themselves fear success

25. When defensive pessimists are allowed to worry about an upcoming test, they _________ than people not allowed to worry.

   a. performed worse
   b. felt better
   c. experienced more anxiety
   d. became more optimistic

Integrative Questions

1. Give your own description of a person with a high need for Achievement. How is need for Achievement like other trait measures? What kinds of careers and jobs are best suited for those with high achievement motivation? Does high need for Achievement always lead to success in the workplace? (204-206)

2. With respect to gender and achievement motivation, what standards of success should researchers apply to achievement settings? Explain how different cultures define success. How might attributions and achievement goals differ in different cultures? (208-209)

3. What kind of people are likely to have a heart attack? What are the three major components of the personality of such people? State the one underlying concept proposed by Glass on which all three dimensions of attribution may rest. Give one piece of evidence to support the idea of one single concept. (214-216)

4. Give two reasons why measures of Type A behavior do not always predict health problems. Explain what is meant by "toxic component" and state whether or not researchers have found it. If so, what is it? (218-220)

5. What are the differences between introversion and shyness? List all of the characteristics you have learned about social anxiety and discuss the relationship of each one to Freud's original conception of anxiety. In other words, give a Freudian explanation that contrasts with the explanations that emerge from the trait approach. (223-227)

6. Contrast the research presented in the text between evaluation apprehension as a cause of social anxiety and other possible causes. What do therapy programs do to help people overcome their shyness? (226-227)

7. In what ways are people with high emotional intensity similar to those with low emotional intensity? What is the relationship between emotional expressiveness and successful romantic relationships, and does this relationship depend on other aspects of emotion such as expressiveness? (231, 234-236)

8. State the advantages and disadvantages of dispositional optimism. What are some of the differences between optimists and pessimists when faced with stressful events? What coping strategies do these two kinds of personalities use? (236-239)

Evaluative Questions

1. Suppose you are looking for a full-time job. Based on your personal assessment of your level of need for Achievement, what kinds of jobs would be a good fit to your personality? List three different occupations in which you can succeed. (205-206)

2. According to research by McClelland, parenting practices can promote achievement motivation. What are some of these practices? Give examples that illustrate the influence of parenting on need for Achievement. Use one example to illustrate that high achievement can be a double-edged sword. (207-208)

3. Suppose you work in human resources for a large company as an interviewer of applicants for jobs. Your task is to determine those applicants who have high need for Achievement. For each of the following interview questions, give a model response of an applicant with high achievement motivation.
    a. What are your career goals?
    b. What have you failed at and how have you handled that failure?
    c. How did you decide to go into this field? (209-214)

4. Think about the most recent exam you had to take in college. Based on your experience on that exam, what attributions do you make for your success or failure? Where do your attributions fall along the three dimensions of stability, locus, and control? What does your self-analysis suggest about your achievement goals? What could it mean for your future behavior in school? (209-214)

5. Consider someone you know who many would agree is a shy person. Identify the situations in which you think the person is most shy. Could evaluation apprehension be the reason for social anxiety? Specify the ways in which the person fits the characteristics of socially anxious people. (223-227)

6. At this very moment, how would you classify your emotional affectivity according to the information presented in Figure 8.3 of the text? To what degree do the dimensions of positive and negative affect have predictive validity? (229)

7. Give examples that illustrate the three aspects of emotion known as affectivity, intensity, and expressiveness. Consider how these qualities of emotion fit into the Big Five Model of personality and write about the relationship. (183, 228-236)

8. From the graph presented in Figure 8.5 of your text, how do optimists and pessimists stack up along the various coping strategies? Give one explanation and one criticism of any pattern to the results of this research. Given how these personalities tend to use different strategies, what can be concluded about the health prospects for both active and avoidance strategy users? (238-240)

Answers to Multiple Choice Questions

1. c, 204
2. b, 205
3. b, 206
4. a, 206
5. d, 207
6. d, 207
7. a, 208
8. b, 208
9. d, 211
10. a, 211
11. c, 212
12. d, 215
13. b, 216
14. c, 217
15. b, 219
16. d, 223
17. d, 225
18. c, 226
19. b, 228
20. a, 230
21. d, 234
22. d, 234
23. c, 237
24. b, 241
25. b, 241

Chapter 9

The Biological Approach

Theory, Application, and Assessment

Hans Eysenck's Theory of Personality

Temperament

Evolutionary Personality Psychology

Application: Children's Temperaments and School

Assessment: Brain Electrical Activity and Cerebral Asymmetry

Strengths and Criticisms of the Biological Approach

Learning Objectives

1. Briefly sketch the history of the study of biological influence on personality. State why the "blank slate" view is no longer supported by psychologists and discuss the reasons for the growing acceptance of biological influences on personality.
2. Describe Eysenck's view of the role of biology in human personality by summarizing his research strategy and discussing his approach to the structure of personality.
3. State the ways in which extraverts and introverts differ and the ways that they are similar. Identify what we now know about cortical arousal and state the second major dimension of Eysenck's model.
4. List and discuss three arguments made by Eysenck for the biological basis of personality.
5. Define temperaments and state where they come from. Discuss how temperaments develop from childhood into adult personality traits and identify the three temperament dimensions that are most widely accepted.
6. State the behavior pattern that temperament researchers find most important. Give specific evidence for the influence of childhood temperament on adult personality.

7. State the basic tenets of evolutionary personality psychology. Describe the role of natural selection and the psychological mechanisms that are thought to determine personality.
8. Explain how human characteristics like anxiety could have evolved. Discuss the role of social exclusion in the evolution of human anxiety.
9. Describe how inhibited and uninhibited children respond to their first day of kindergarten. Define and contrast the three basic patterns of behavior in school children derived from nine temperamental differences.
10. Discuss the impact of temperament on how well a child performs in school, including three basic reasons for the relationship.
11. Explain what is meant by the Goodness of Fit Model and provide a strategy for improving teaching based on it.
12. Discuss the nature of EEG research on personality and emotion and describe cerebral asymmetry. Explain how emotion is predicted by individual differences in cerebral asymmetry and the possible role of thresholds in brain activity.
13. Give three strengths of the biological approach to personality. State how this approach serves as a bridge between personality psychology and biology.
14. Summarize the criticisms that can be made of the biological approach to personality. State whether each criticism is a methodological limitation or a general theoretical consideration.

Important Concepts

specific response level (p. 247)
habitual response level (p. 247)
extraversion (p. 247)
supertrait (p. 247)
neuroticism (p. 247)
emotionality (p. 254)
activity (p. 254)
psychoticism (p. 256)
inhibited children (p. 258)
uninhibited children (p. 258)
anxiety to novelty (p. 259)
evolutionary personality theory (p. 261)
psychological mechanisms (p. 262)
natural selection (p. 262)
easy child (p. 265)
difficult child (p. 265)
slow-to-warm-up child (p. 265)
Goodness of Fit Model (p. 267)
electroencephalograph (p. 268)
alpha wave (p. 269)
cerebral asymmetry (p. 270)

InfoTrac *Search terms:*

Hans Eysenck (p. 250)
temperament (p. 253)
sociability (p. 254)
social exclusion (p. 263)
EEG (p. 268)

Programmed Review

There is a growing recognition that personality cannot be separated from ________ factors.

biological p. 246

At Eysenck's second level of personality structure are "traits" that he referred to as ________ .

habitual responses p. 247

Eysenck argued that extraverts and introverts differ both in their behavior and in their ________ makeup.

physiological p. 248

Today researchers describe extraverts and introverts in terms of their different sensitivity to ________ .

stimulation p. 249

From all of the evidence he gathered and intuition, Eysenck estimated that about ________ of the variance in personality is accounted for by biological factors.

two-thirds p. 253

Temperament researchers argue that both genetic predispositions and the ________ influence the course of personality development.

environment p. 253

People who are easily upset or have a quick temper are high in ________ .

emotionality p. 254

Parents of ________ children can do their child a favor by becoming sensitive to the child's discomfort in unfamiliar settings.

inhibited p. 260

Proponents of evolutionary personality theory use the process of ________ to explain universal human characteristics.

natural selection p. 261

Some members of a species possess inherited characteristics that help them survive and reproduce, with the net result of _________ features.

species-specific p. 262

Compared to the easy child and slow-to-warm-up child, the _________ child is typically low in adaptability and in a negative mood.

difficult p. 265

Opportunities for learning and achievement in school may be shaped by the child's _________ .

temperament p. 266

Differences in temperament can influence a student's grades depending on the teacher's _________ .

expectations and demands p. 267

Researchers measure brain activity with an instrument called an _________ .

electroencephalograph (EEG) p. 268

The difference in right and left hemisphere activity is referred to as _________ by researchers.

cerebral asymmetry p. 270

Some researchers explain findings of cerebral asymmetry in terms of _________ for positive and negative mood.

thresholds p. 271

With respect to emotional disorders, depressed people have been shown to have more brain activation on the _________ than normals.

right side p. 271

One of the most important messages from the biological approach is that we need to be more aware of the _________ on how much we can change personality.

limitations p. 274

Multiple Choice Questions

1. The growing acceptance of the biological influences on personality is partly

   a. due to a return to the notion of the blank slate.
   b. a reflection of the decline of psychoanalysis in academic psychology.
   c. a reflection of behaviorism's decline in academic psychology.
   d. due to computer technology of the late twentieth century.

2. According to Hans Eysenck's model of personality structure, the level that consists of individual behaviors is called the ___________ level.

   a. habitual response
   b. conditioned response
   c. specific response
   d. none of the above

3. Sherry has many friends and enjoys purchasing gifts for them on impulse. She gets excited when she surprises her friends with these gifts. Her behavior suggests that she is at the high end on the _________ supertrait dimension.

   a. extraversion
   b. neuroticism
   c. psychoticism
   d. sentimentalism

4. Using factor analysis, Eysenck found that people who score high on the dimension of psychoticism tend to be

   a. egocentric and aggressive.
   b. impulsive.
   c. not generally concerned with the rights and welfare of others.
   d. all of the above

5. Among the arguments Eysenck made for the influence of biology on personality, which of the following was *not* included?

   a. the consistency of neuroticism over time
   b. results from cross-cultural research
   c. the important role of genetics in determining the level of introversion
   d. both a and b

6. Which of the following is *not* a basic temperament according to Buss and Plomin?

   a. activity
   b. connectivity
   c. emotionality
   d. sociability

7. Tonya is a three-year-old who accompanies her mother at a new place, her mother's dentist's office. While in the waiting room Tonya sees several new people and is handed a toy that she has never seen before. According to Kagan and his colleagues, if Tonya is an inhibited child, then she will likely react to these circumstances with

   a. interest.
   b. fear.
   c. curiosity.
   d. anxiety.

8. Inhibited children are vulnerable to a specific form of anxiety generated by unfamiliar people, settings, or challenges. This form of anxiety is called

   a. anxiety to novelty.
   b. neurotic fear.
   c. moral anxiety.
   d. neurotic phobia.

9. Evidence for the biological basis of temperament includes which of the following physical differences researchers have found between inhibited and uninhibited children almost from the moment of birth?

   a. susceptibility to allergies
   b. body build
   c. eye color
   d. all of the above

10. When researchers measured children's fear of unfamiliar situations at 21 months and again at four years of age, the children were brought back to the laboratory at five and a half years and the researchers found

    a. the children who were inhibited earlier displayed more risky behavior when playing a ball-tossing game.
    b. the children who were inhibited earlier displayed more risky behavior when playing on a mattress in a falling game.
    c. that children who were inhibited at 21 months and four years again clung to their mother or father as before.
    d. that children who were uninhibited at 21 months and four years began to cling to their mother or father at five and a half years.

11. Proponents of evolutionary personality theory use the process of natural selection to explain

    a. neuroticism.
    b. the human libido.
    c. universal human characteristics.
    d. both b and c

12. According to evolutionary personality psychologists, social exclusion leads to anxiety because

    a. people fear that others will punish them.
    b. each of us are reminded of a traumatic experience in childhood.
    c. experiencing anxiety serves an important survival function.
    d. all of the above

13. Among the psychological mechanisms identified by evolutionary psychologists as resulting from the natural selection process is

    a. arrogance.
    b. anger.
    c. ambivalence.
    d. all of the above

14. Arguments given for the evolution of anxiety include all but which of the following?

    a. a need to belong to groups
    b. a need to dominate others
    c. anxiety is found in nearly all cultures
    d. anxiety meets the survival needs of the species

15. Which of the following is *not* a temperamental difference found to affect how a child performs in school?

    a. approach or withdrawal
    b. distractibility
    c. attention to details
    d. adaptability

16. Larry is in kindergarten and shows signs of being inhibited. He is reluctant to engage in new activities and slow to adapt to new tasks given by his teacher. Larry is probably

    a. an easy child.
    b. a slow-to-warm-up child.
    c. a difficult child.
    d. a fast-to-cool-down child.

17. Students get higher grades and better evaluations from teachers when

    a. the student's temperament matches the teacher's expectations.
    b. the student's interests match the teacher's interests and focus.
    c. the student's temperament leads to strong attention to details.
    d. the student's temperament supports moral values.

18. Sarah is a grade school teacher who is faced with a variety of student capabilities in her class. According to the Goodness of Fit Model, a good teaching strategy for Sarah would be

    a. to focus on the students with high ability and request they assist the others.
    b. to present lessons and assignments that fit with what her students enjoy.
    c. to optimize learning by matching assignments and tasks with individual students' learning styles.
    d. to ignore different temperaments and hold high standards of academic performance for all.

19. Which of the following is false about differences in temperament patterns in children?

    a. Differences show up on teachers' evaluations.
    b. Differences are found in the child's grades.
    c. Differences are found in scores on achievement tests.
    d. Differences are related to intelligence.

20. Which of the following is an advantage of using the electroencephalograph (EEG)?

    a. It allows researchers to record brain activity in long intervals.
    b. The electrode paste that is used is not messy.
    c. The procedure is not uncomfortable.
    d. It is a complex procedure that allows the participant's hair to grow back.

21. Using the electroencephalograph (EEG), researchers have found higher activation in the left hemisphere is associated with

    a. smiling.
    b. negative mood.
    c. greater reactions to films that elicit fear.
    d. feelings of disgust.

22. A strength of the biological approach is that

    a. it has succeeded in identifying specific parameters for psychologists who want to change behavior.
    b. there seems to be no limit to psychologists' ability to test for biological factors.
    c. most of its advocates are medical doctors with an interest in treating disease.
    d. it makes a variety of suggestions for personality change.

Integrative Questions

1. How does a complete understanding of human personality require us to go beyond the traditional boundaries of personality psychology? Specify how Eysenck's theory goes beyond those traditional boundaries. What aspects of his theory depart from the Freudian approach and the trait approach? In what ways is Eysenck's theory related to these? (247-251)

2. Discuss how the three general dispositions described by Buss and Plomin translate into adult personality traits. Include in your discussion how the environment plays a role in this development. Does the research on trait stability in children support the three-dimension model? (254-261)

3. From the discussion of childhood temperaments given in the text, summarize what parents can do to help their inhibited children. Speculate on what teachers can do to improve the education of inhibited children. (257-261)

4. List the psychological mechanisms given in the text that have been identified as resulting from the natural selection process and give the logic behind the idea that each is adaptive for survival. How do these mechanisms interact with experience? (261-264)

5. Give an example of how a classroom can be arranged to be more helpful for students with different temperaments. Give examples of how teachers can misinterpret temperamental differences in students and how they can overcome misinterpretations by awareness of the origins of temperaments. (266-268)

6. Write a story titled, "The day I was a subject in a study of personality," that describes what would take place if you participated in a study in which your brain activity was measured. Include what you would be thinking and feeling and what the likely results would be. (268-272)

Evaluative Questions

1. What temperaments do you possess? Give personal evidence for your own emotionality, activity, and sociability. Do you think these temperaments were inherited? Why or why not? (253-257)

2. Describe one study that provides evidence that the temperaments a person has in childhood show up later in life. Consider at least one factor other than temperaments that may explain the results of the study. State how it could. (257-261)

3. Specify where evolutionary theory and the Freudian approach cross paths. If Freud were alive in the latter part of the twentieth century, do you think he would have agreed with evolutionary personality theory? Why or why not? (261-264)

4. State a definition of the behavior pattern psychologists call altruism. Given that the expression of altruism often results in the sacrifice of one's life, how might an evolutionary personality psychologist explain altruism as a result of natural selection? (Hint: Humans share many genes with siblings and other family members.) (261-262)

5. Given that anxiety generally prevents humans from behaviors that would lead to social eclusion, can we be absolutely sure that anxiety is a biologically based factor in human personality? Consider the kinds of arguments made by evolutionary personality psychologists for the existence of anxiety. (262-264)

6. Consider the mix of students in your personality class with you. Do you think the temperamental patterns of childhood are still represented to some extent in the young adults in your class? Discuss how far some grade school teachers might go to change their teaching style to be sensitive to those children who are slow to warm up to new tasks. Do the professors at your school show an awareness that not all college students approach school and learning in the same way? (264-268)

7. State one criticism of measuring brain activity with the EEG as a means of assessing personality. Given the findings on thresholds given in the text, what are the implications of these data for Eysenck's theory of personality? (247, 268-272)

Answers to Multiple Choice Questions

1.	c, 246	12.	c, 263
2.	c, 247	13.	b, 262
3.	a, 249	14.	b, 263
4.	d, 251	15.	c, 264
5.	a, 251	16.	b, 265
6.	b, 254	17.	a, 267
7.	d, 258	18.	c, 267
8.	a, 259	19.	d, 266
9.	d, 259	20.	c, 269
10.	c, 259	21.	a, 270
11.	c, 261	22.	a, 272

Chapter 10

The Biological Approach

Relevant Research

Heritability of Personality Traits

Extraversion-Introversion

Evolutionary Personality Theory and Mate Selection

Learning Objectives

1. Discuss the heritability of personality traits and the common methods used by researchers to separate environmental influences from genetic influences on personality.
2. Specifically discuss the rationale behind the twin-study method and adoption studies of genetic influence. Give the general findings regarding the contribution of genetic influences on personality. List and describe the problems associated with each of these methods of genetic research.
3. Discuss the heritability of extraversion and review the two main causes of individual differences in extraversion-introversion. Present various sources of evidence that suggest these differences are based in biology.
4. Describe the relationship between extraversion and preferred level of arousal. Give the research evidence in support of this relationship.
5. State who is happier among extraverts and introverts and discuss several reasons for this difference.
6. Discuss the kinds of information researchers have found about gender roles and the nature of romantic relationships. Define parental investment and present the different ideas men and women have about it.

7. Contrast the basis of mate selection for males with that for females by explaining the different evolutionary motives men and women have in choosing a mate.
8. Discuss what men look for in women and describe the research that supports the evolutionary basis of mate selection in men. Discuss what women look for in men and describe the research that supports the evolutionary basis of mate selection in women.
9. List the conclusions that can be drawn about gender differences in mate selection and then discuss the limitations faced by evolutionary personality researchers who study these differences.

Important Concepts

monozygotic (MZ) twins (p. 280)
dizygotic (DZ) twins (p. 280)
nonadditive effects (p. 284)
parental investment (p. 292)
intrasexual selection (p. 293)

InfoTrac *Search terms:*

twin-study method (p. 280)
extraversion (p. 285)
subjective well-being (p. 289)
personality and mate selection (p. 291)

Programmed Review

One reason for the resistance by psychologists to acknowledge the important role of biology in human personality is that the _________ view has such great appeal.

blank slate p. 276

For both technological reasons and ethical reasons, it is not possible to _________ people's genes and observe the kind of adult they become.

manipulate p. 279

The most popular method used to examine the role of genetics and the environment in personality is the _________ method.

twin-study p. 280

Two babies that come from different fertilized eggs may simply be siblings or ________ .

dizygotic twins p. 280

The most problematic assumption in adoption studies is that parents treat their adopted child ________ they do their biological offspring.

in the same way p. 284

The genetic influence of some personality traits may not be seen unless a ________ of more than one gene is inherited.

unique combination p. 284

Each person born with an introvert will develop a heightened ________ to stimulation.

sensitivity p. 288

When given the opportunity, research participants who are introverts tend to set earphones at ________ levels than extraverts.

lower p. 289

On average, extraverts report higher levels of subjective ________ than introverts.

well-being p. 289

Researchers have found that every day of the week extraverts tend to have a better __________ than introverts.

mood p. 290

The result of ________ is that extraverts experience more mood swings than introverts.

impulsivity p. 291

From the evolutionary perspective, choosing a romantic partner is based in part on concerns for ________ .

parental investment p. 292

The evidence is abundant that men are more likely than women to look at _________ when selecting a dating or marriage partner.

physical attractiveness p. 293

According to the parental investment analysis, women prefer to mate with men who will be able to _________ their offspring.

provide for p. 296

Many learned preferences for romantic partners may _________ inherited instincts.

overshadow p. 300

Multiple Choice Questions

1. The question of the origin of personality between genetics and the environment is *not* which of these shapes our personality *but* rather

    a. why we have personalities in the first place.
    b. who has the better theory of personality development.
    c. what traits can be changed by changing the environment.
    d. to what extent our personalities are shaped by each.

2. Siblings' personalities may be similar because

    a. children inherited personality traits from their parents.
    b. siblings share the same living environments during childhood.
    c. siblings are raised in the same way by parents.
    d. all of the above

3. Twins that we commonly call identical twins

    a. are monozygotic.
    b. are dizygotic.
    c. come from different fertilized eggs.
    d. are sometimes called fraternal twins.

4. Behavior genetics researchers have taken their data from twin studies and used formulas to estimate that about _________ of the stability in adult personalities can be attributed to genetics.

   a. 10%
   b. 20%
   c. 30%
   d. 40%

5. Which of the following is a problem for the assumption that MZ and DZ twins are raised in equally similar environments?

   a. DZ twins may be treated more alike than identical twins.
   b. MZ twins purposefully join different clubs and have different friends.
   c. MZ twins may share more of their environment than DZ twins.
   d. all of the above

6. Adoptions are not __________ events.

   a. important
   b. controllable
   c. random
   d. comparable

7. One problem with adoption studies is that the homes in which twins are placed

   a. are so very different that comparisons cannot be made.
   b. are often very similar because families who adopt children are similar in important ways.
   c. are highly specialized for adoptive parenting.
   d. allow the same genetic influences to emerge.

8. The genetic influence of some personality traits may not be seen unless a specific combination of genes in inherited. Such complex influences are known as

   a. monozygotic influences.
   b. combinatorial effects.
   c. nonadditive effects.
   d. genetic correlations.

9. Research on the genetic heritability of extraversion-introversion has made use of

   a. brain activity measures.
   b. the twin-study method.
   c. differences in sensitivity to stimulation.
   d. only twins that have been reared together (in the same environment).

10. Research has found that students who prefer a quiet, isolated room were more likely to be

    a. introverts.
    b. extraverts.
    c. neurotics.
    d. of no particular personality.

11. A study of the library rooms preferred by different students demonstrated that

    a. students in a quiet and isolated room were more likely to be extraverts.
    b. when in the library even introverts prefer the opportunity to socialize.
    c. extraverts preferred open rooms more than isolated rooms.
    d. introverts preferred to study in rooms close to an exit.

12. Susan spends much of her time visiting friends and going to parties. Although she feels less positive about her mood on Monday than on Friday night, Susan

    a. is an introvert and will likely decline in mood by Saturday.
    b. is an extravert and will likely decline in mood by Saturday.
    c. is an extravert who likely experiences more positive mood throughout the week than an introvert.
    d. is an extravert and will likely experience less positive mood on Monday than an introvert.

13. The fact that friends often serve as an important buffer against stress supports the idea that extraverts

    a. are generally more anxious than introverts.
    b. have higher positive affect due to greater social activity.
    c. are less sensitive to information about rewards than introverts.
    d. often find interacting with friends an unpleasant experience.

14. Why might extraverts not always be happier than introverts?

    a. Extraverts are more likely to be socially active.
    b. Extraverts are more likely to be impulsive.
    c. Introverts do not involve themselves in activities that increase feelings of competence and worth.
    d. Extraverts are more sensitive to positive feedback.

15. Which of the following is true about parental investment?

    a. Males are more selective about whom they choose to mate than females.
    b. Males of many species are free to mate with as many females as they can.
    c. Investment in selecting a mate is larger for males than for females.
    d. Males select mates who are more likely to be good parents.

16. If you surveyed 100 men about the features in women they consider to be important for selecting a wife, which of the following items would be the most likely result?

    a. Men identify intelligence less frequently than women.
    b. Men identify ambition more often than attractiveness.
    c. The most frequent feature identified is nurturing.
    d. The most frequent feature identified is good looks.

17. According to parental investment analysis, women prefer to mate with dominant men

    a. because they often have more material resources.
    b. only if they are willing to provide for the welfare of their children.
    c. only if they have material resources to share.
    d. because they are loud and brutish and put it on display.

18. One result of human males' preferences in mate selection is

    a. women compete for a man's attention.
    b. women compete in the workplace.
    c. women brag about their sexual encounters.
    d. all of the above

19. A result of patterns of mate selection by human females is that

    a. men seldom let on what their financial resources may be.
    b. men alter their physical appearance to be more attractive to women.
    c. men compete for a woman's attention.
    d. all of the above

20. With regard to mate selection, one limitation of evolutionary personality theory is that

    a. instincts inherited from our ancestors may overshadow the characteristics men and women look for in some cultures.
    b. the methods do not give researchers the ability to make strong predictions.
    c. researchers cannot manipulate the variables they study.
    d. it assumes a causal relationship between mate selection and environment.

Integrative Questions

1. In general, how much of our personalities are inherited from our parents? Describe the logic behind two methods researchers use to determine the heritability of personality traits. (277-283)

2. What assumptions are made about twins that allow researchers to study the biological contributions to personality? Of these assumptions, which are called into question by critics of the biological approach to personality? Discuss four problems associated with genetics research. (280, 283-285)

3. Discuss the research evidence for the heritability of the extraversion. What features of the Swedish and Finnish samples make them so important for genetics researchers? Specify how the twin-study method is used in these studies. (285-287)

4. Discuss the difference in preference for arousal between extraverts and introverts. Give two ways in which sensitivity to stimulation translates into behavior. If you spoke with Eysenck, what would he say about the genetic research on the heritability of the extraversion trait? (288-289, 247-249)

5. In two columns list what men look for in women and what women look for in men. Give the evolutionary reasons for the contrast in the two columns. What other evidence can be given in support of evolutionary personality theory in addition to selection based on features of high reproductive value? (292-298)

6. Give an example of one cultural norm that interferes with the predictions of evolutionary psychology about mate selection. (297)

Evaluative Questions

1. Discuss the logic behind the common methods used by genetics researchers to estimate the heritability of personality. List and discuss the various problems with these procedures, including the way in which heritability estimates are undermined by each problem. (283-285)

2. At this moment as you study, do you have the stereo or TV on or off? Or if you are not near a stereo or television, do you prefer some noise or no noise when you are studying? According to research on sensitivity to stimulation, what does your study environment preference tell you about your personality? (288-289)

3. Who is happier, introverts or extraverts? State the evidence that supports your answer. Discuss one alternative explanation for the differences in reported level of positive mood and give a rule of thumb for obtaining happiness. (289-291)

4. How might the evolutionary perspective explain the mate selection of homosexual men and women? (291-298)

5. Critically evaluate the findings of the evolutionary perspective on mate selection, stating if you think the evidence is weak or strong and why. What are the major limitations to this research? (291-300)

6. Consider the characteristics in men that women look for when selecting a partner. In your opinion, which characteristics do not strictly fit the evolutionary perspective in modern society? Give reasons for these departures from the predictions of evolutionary psychology. (292-299)

Answers to Multiple Choice Questions

1. d, 277
2. d, 280
3. a, 280
4. d, 281
5. c, 283
6. c, 284
7. b, 284
8. c, 284
9. b, 286
10. a, 288
11. c, 288
12. c, 290
13. b, 290
14. b, 291
15. b, 292
16. d, 293
17. b, 297
18. a, 293
19. c, 297
20. c, 299

Chapter 11

The Humanistic Approach

Theory, Application, and Assessment

The Roots of Humanistic Psychology

Key Elements of the Humanistic Approach

Carl Rogers

Abraham Maslow

The Psychology of Optimal Experience

Application: Person-Centered Therapy and Job Satisfaction

Assessment: The Q-Sort Technique

Strengths and Criticisms of the Humanistic Approach

Learning Objectives

1. Present the historical roots of humanistic psychology, discussing its relation to earlier approaches to personality and its philosophical influences. Include in the discussion what is meant by "third force" in American psychology.
2. List and briefly explain the four key elements of the humanistic approach to personality. Specify why each is important to humanistic psychologists.
3. Discuss the basic tenets of Carl Rogers's humanistic approach to personality. Describe his characterization of the fully functioning person.
4. Explain where anxiety comes from according to Rogers. Discuss the defenses that Rogers suggested we use against anxiety.
5. Define conditions of worth according to Rogers and specify the importance of what he called unconditional positive regard for the person's self-concept.

6. Discuss the central concepts of Abraham Maslow's theory of personality. Contrast his conception of the human with the view of Sigmund Freud. List and define each of the five levels in Maslow's hierarchy of needs.
7. Define self-actualization and discuss the common misconceptions people have about Maslow's need hierarchy.
8. Describe how Maslow went about studying psychologically healthy people. List each of the characteristics of the individual who is self-actualized according to Maslow and define peak experience.
9. Discuss the concept of optimal experience. List and define the eight characteristics of optimal experiences identified by Csikszentmihalyi. Specify what everyday activities are more likely to be flow experiences.
10. Describe the person-centered approach to psychotherapy. Indicate the significance of the proper relationship in the therapeutic setting by discussing the elements that Rogers suggested are necessary for a therapeutic relationship to exist.
11. Explain how Maslow's need hierarchy can be used to account for job satisfaction. Discuss the idea of Eupsychian management promoted by Maslow.
12. Describe the Q-Sort technique of personality assessment and explain how it is used to track progress during psychotherapy. Discuss the different correlational outcomes of the Q-Sort depending on the agreement of clients' real and ideal selves.
13. Discuss the specific influences that the humanistic approach to personality has had on the field of psychology in general and psychotherapy in particular.
14. Present five different criticisms that have been made of the humanistic approach. Discuss why the usefulness of humanistic psychotherapy is limited and its effectiveness often questioned.

Important Concepts

"third force" (p. 303)
phenomenological psychology (p. 303)
existential psychologists (p. 304)
existential anxiety (p. 304)
personal responsibility (p. 305)
the here and now (p. 305)
person-centered approach (p. 307)
fully functioning (p. 307)
personal growth (p. 307)
subception (p. 310)
denial (p. 310)
distortion (p. 310)
disorganization (p. 311)
conditions of worth (p. 311)
conditional positive regard (p. 311)
unconditional positive regard (p. 312)
deficiency motive (p. 314)
growth needs (p. 314)
belongingness and love needs (p. 315)
physiological needs (p. 315)
safety needs (p. 315)
esteem needs (p. 316)

(continued on next page)

need for self-actualization (p. 316)
enculturalization (p. 319)
peak experiences (p. 319)
self-actualizing creativity (p. 319)
optimal experience (p. 321)
flow (p. 321)
person-centered therapy (p. 324)
reflection (p. 325)
Eupsychian management (p. 327)
real self (p. 328)
ideal self (p. 328)
Q-Sort (p. 328)
positive psychology (p. 332)

InfoTrac *Search terms:*

humanistic psychology (p. 303)
self-actualization (p. 307)
Carl Rogers (p. 308)
Abraham Maslow (p. 313)
hierarchy of needs (p. 314)

Programmed Review

Important aspects of human personality such as __________ were missing from the Freudian and behavioristic approaches.

free will and human dignity p. 303

Existential psychologists focused on __________, which are feelings of dread and panic that stem from a realization that there is no meaning to one's life.

existential anxiety p. 304

According to Carl Rogers, individuals progress toward an ultimate satisfying state of being _________ .

fully functioning p. 307

Rogers pioneered humanistic psychotherapy with his _________ approach.

person-centered p. 307

If information is threatening to our self-concept, Rogers suggested the information is processed by _________ rather than perception.

subception p. 310

The most common defense, according to Rogers, is the process of _________ .

distortion p. 310

An example of conditional positive regard is when a parent loves their children only when the children do what is _________ of them.

expected p. 311

The second level of Maslow's hierarchy is the _________ needs.

safety p. 315

Maslow believed very few people reach __________, which is the point at which their potential is fully developed.

self-actualization p. 317

Because of their self-acceptance, self-actualized people do not feel _________ about the bad things they have done.

guilty p. 319

A _________ takes place when time and place are transcended and one loses anxieties and experiences a unity of self with the universe.

peak experience p. 319

People report that during optimal experiences they feel as if they are caught in natural and __________ movement from one step to the next.

effortless p. 321

In person-centered therapy, the therapist's job is to allow the client to get back on a __________ and to continue progressing.

positive growth track p. 324

Maslow's work has influenced the way many ___________ look at job satisfaction.

job counselors/employers p. 327

In a correlational analysis of Q-Sort responses, a zero correlation indicates that the client's real and ideal selves are __________ .

completely unrelated p. 330

Multiple Choice Questions

1. Emphasis on _________ in the 1960s provided fertile soil for the growth of humanistic psychology.

    a. civil rights
    b. individuality
    c. communism
    d. laboratory rats

2. For Abraham Maslow, the turning point in his thinking about human personality came while he was

    a. watching a World War II parade.
    b. wondering about therapists' abilities to decide for patients what their problems were and how to solve them.
    c. listening to a lecture on psychoanalysis.
    d. playing in a football game in college.

3. Which of the following is *not* a key element of humanistic psychology?

    a. personal responsibility
    b. identity crisis
    c. personal growth
    d. none of the above

4. Whereas psychoanalysts emphasize that adult personalities are formed in childhood, humanistic therapists focus on

    a. the individual and the group.
    b. the potential and future.
    c. the bold and the beautiful.
    d. the here and now.

5. When William approached the beautiful Carol and asked her out on a date, she laughed at him and then walked away. To handle this rejection, William convinced himself that Carol really didn't turn him down but rather she was laughing at something else. Which defense against anxiety does William's behavior illustrate?

    a. distortion
    b. denial
    c. displacement
    d. disorganization

6. Which of the following is a characteristic of the fully functioning person, according to Rogers?

    a. They are open to their experiences.
    b. They trust their own feelings.
    c. They pay attention to what is happening in the here and now.
    d. all of the above

7. According to Maslow, the motive that results from a lack of some object is called a __________ motive.

    a. hierarchy
    b. envy
    c. deficiency
    d. possession

8. If you were shipwrecked and landed on a tropical island, you would most likely _________ first.

    a. look for inhabitants
    b. build a safe shelter
    c. establish a form of self-government
    d. look for food and fresh water

9. Among the common misconceptions of Maslow's need hierarchy is the assumption that

    a. all needs are included at some level in the need hierarchy.
    b. how well our lower needs are satisfied determines how much those needs influence our behavior.
    c. our lower needs must be satisfied totally before we can turn to higher needs.
    d. all cultures have the same basic need hierarchy.

10. Self-actualized people tend to

    a. be more spontaneous.
    b. ignore their own weaknesses and focus on their personal strengths.
    c. show higher acceptance of other people for who they are.
    d. be more greatly inhibited in their social interactions.

11. Sam has fulfilled his belongingness needs by falling in love and getting married to the woman of his dreams. This means that

    a. it is now time to work on his need for self-actualization.
    b. Sam would never have become self-actualized without getting married.
    c. it is now time to work on his esteem needs.
    d. none of the above

12. People lose their anxieties and experience a unity of self with the universe during

    a. peak experiences.
    b. moments of self-actualizing creativity.
    c. moments of emotional growth.
    d. optimal experiences.

13. When Csikszentmihalyi asked people to identify a moment when they felt most alive, participants in his study said that

    a. the task they were engaged in was challenging.
    b. the experience involved a task that demanded the person's full concentration.
    c. each step in the experience seemed to flow automatically to the next.
    d. all of the above

14. According to Rogers, the proper therapeutic relationship between therapist and client includes which of the following?

    a. a peak experience during therapy
    b. unconscious impulses being revealed
    c. transference
    d. unconditional positive regard

15. During person-centered therapy the therapist offers ___________ of what the client seems to be saying.

    a. an analysis
    b. an interpretation
    c. a restatement
    d. his or her advice on the topic

16. When are people more likely to experience flow?

    a. on a vacation from work
    b. in the middle of the day
    c. when learning is easy
    d. when working at one's job

17. Rogers believed that research into how people change during psychotherapy would help therapists

    a. estimate the limitations of their approach.
    b. become more sensitive to the needs of patients.
    c. uncover the parental influences on the personality.
    d. improve their ability to work with clients.

18. Which of the following is *not* a component of the optimal experience?

    a. Satisfaction is received from a task.
    b. The activity has clear goals.
    c. One can concentrate only on the task at hand.
    d. Attention is absorbed by the activity.

19. The use of the Q-Sort technique of personality assessment fits nicely with Rogers's theory of personality because

    a. clients know themselves best.
    b. therapists must help clients place the cards into the correct categories.
    c. clients discover the unrealistic ways in which they see themselves.
    d. clients must be told how to behave more appropriately by their therapist.

20. One criticism of the humanistic approach to personality is that many key concepts

    a. offer little that can be applied to education.
    b. have outlived their usefulness in modern society.
    c. are poorly defined.
    d. only apply to wealthy individuals.

Integrative Questions

1. If the humanistic approach to personality is the "third force" in American psychology, what were the first and second forces? Carefully contrast these "forces" by emphasizing their similarities and differences in theory, application, and assessment. (303-304)

2. Contrast Rogers's view of human beings with Freud's conception of the person. Give an example of conditional positive regard and an example of unconditional positive regard. (307-312, 49-55)

3. Give an example of each level of Maslow's hierarchy of needs. Define enculturalization and peak experiences. With which approach would you contrast Maslow's view of personality the most? What theorist agrees with Maslow the most and why? (312-316, 319-320)

4. What makes people happy according to Csikszentmihalyi? Discuss each of the characteristics of optimal experiences and state which personality trait should correspond to frequency in these. Write about someone you know whose personality does not conform to the expectation. (320-323, 289-291)

5. Give an assumption from Rogers's theory that involves the unconscious. In what respects is the process similar to Freudian conceptions of the mind? (310, 49-51)

6. Describe a typical person-centered therapeutic session in which the client is given the Q-Sort assessment. What are the general steps involved in the technique? What will the therapist discover about the client by using this technique? (324-326, 328-331)

Evaluative Questions

1. Consider the basic assumptions of humanistic psychology. Discuss the importance of a person's uniqueness in this approach to personality. Given that most personality researchers attempt to discover the underlying structure and general influences on personality rather than one's uniqueness, how can humanistic psychology be considered a useful approach to personality? (305-307)

2. Identify a person you know who is self-actualized or typically behaves in a self-actualized manner. What specific characteristics of this person point to self-actualization? Must the person in the example you gave have all the lower needs completely satisfied? (316-318)

3. Describe an experience that you have had of "flow." How did you feel at that moment? Identify which of the eight components of optimal experience you experienced in your example. Describe a plan for making your work tasks a source of happiness. (320-322)

4. Suppose you were a manager in a large manufacturing company. Given what you now know about Maslow's theory of personality and the hierarchy of needs, what could you do to help satisfy the needs of your employees? If a worker said that she liked the money but was otherwise unhappy with her job, what would you want to know about the worker? (326-327)

5. Consider the several criticisms of the humanistic approach. Do you agree with each criticism or do you feel that there still is a place in psychology for the humanistic view? What aspects of human nature are addressed by humanistic psychology that are not dealt with by any other approach? (331-334)

Answers to Multiple Choice Questions

1.	b, 303
2.	a, 304
3.	b, 305
4.	d, 305
5.	b, 310
6.	d, 307
7.	c, 314
8.	d, 315
9.	c, 318
10.	a, 319
11.	d, 319
12.	a, 319
13.	d, 321
14.	d, 325
15.	c, 325
16.	d, 321
17.	d, 328
18.	a, 322
19.	a, 329
20.	c, 333

Chapter 12

The Humanistic Approach

Relevant Research

Self-Disclosure

Loneliness

Self-Esteem

Solitude

Learning Objectives

1. Summarize the reasons for the initial interest in humanistic psychology and explain why critics of the approach call it "soft" psychology. List four concepts from humanistic psychology that have been highly researched.
2. Discuss the concept of self-disclosure and the implications of the research on self-disclosure for humanistic psychology. Give an example of the rule of disclosure reciprocity and specify the relationship between self-disclosure and feelings of attraction and trust.
3. Explain the role self-disclosure plays in the development of friendships and romantic relationships. Specify the health benefits of disclosing traumatic experiences and the implications of self-disclosure for psychotherapy.
4. Describe how patterns of self-disclosure can vary as a function of gender and by the nature of what an individual is talking about.
5. Contrast loneliness with isolation and give an example of each. Present some explanations humanistic psychologists give for why loneliness is such a widespread problem in America.

6. State how loneliness is measured. Discuss some of the causes of loneliness and the characteristics of lonely people, including the nature of the interactive style lonely people take on and the relative amount of self-disclosure between lonely people and people who are not lonely.
7. Distinguish between self-esteem and self-concept. Discuss the relative importance of self-esteem for humanistic psychologists and their work. Distinguish between global and domain-specific self-esteem.
8. Compare how high self-esteem people and low self-esteem people react to failure. Present some explanations for why these two kinds of people react differently.
9. Discuss the motives that distinguish high and low self-esteem people, including concerns for self-enhancement and self-protection. Explain the self-handicapping strategy and the reason for its use.
10. Define self-esteem stability. Give reasons why some people have feelings about themselves that fluctuate while the feelings of others are more stable.
11. State the reasons why we should rethink our notions of self-esteem when working with other cultures. Discuss implications of different conceptualizations of the self in different cultures.
12. Give the humanistic approach's explanation for why some people desire solitude. Discuss the research findings on solitude and contrast the drawbacks and benefits of solitude.
13. Define preference for solitude and describe people at either end of this individual difference dimension. Discuss the method and results of Burger's research on preference for solitude.

Important Concepts

"soft" psychology (p. 337)
transparent self (p. 339)
dyadic effect (p. 341)
disclosure reciprocity (p. 341)
negative expectations (p. 351)
global self-esteem (p. 355)
domain-specific self-esteem (p. 355)
feelings of self-worth (p. 355)
self-enhancement (p. 359)
self-protection (p. 359)
self-esteem stability (p. 360)
Experience Sampling Method (p. 365)
preference for solitude (p. 368)

InfoTrac *Search terms:*

self-disclosure (p. 339)
loneliness (p. 348)
self-concept (p. 355)
self-esteem (p. 355)
self-handicapping (p. 360)

Programmed Review

In the early years of the third force, humanistic psychologists argued that people cannot be reduced to a set of _________ .

numbers p. 337

People engage in self-disclosure when they reveal _________ information about themselves to another person.

intimate p. 339

Occasionally parents teach us the rules of social interaction directly, but often we are not aware of how we _________ what is expected and what is not appropriate when interacting with others.

learned p. 341

The amount of self-disclosure in a _________ is a strong predictor of satisfaction in it.

marriage p. 343

Research has shown that the more people talk about a tragedy like the death of a spouse, the fewer _________ they have.

health problems p. 344

Loneliness has become _________ on college campuses.

epidemic p. 348

Lonely people tend to approach social interactions with overly _________ expectations for how the encounter will go.

pessimistic p. 351

Given the opportunity to be in a conversation, lonely people tend to take on a _________ role.

passive interpersonal p. 354

In contrast to low self-esteem people, when faced with failure people with high self-esteem typically work _________ as they do after successes.

just as hard p. 356

Some researchers have proposed that people high in self-esteem are motivated by a concern for _________ .

self-enhancement p. 359

In addition to individual differences in level of self-esteem, people may differ in self-esteem _________ .

stability p. 360

In Western societies the concept of high self-esteem is related to what one does to _________ oneself.

distinguish p. 362

Fitting in and doing one's duty are sources of self-satisfaction in _________ cultures.

collectivist p. 363

One reason why some people desire to spend time alone is the _________ style Karen Horney described as "moving away from people."

neurotic p. 365

While they may be the warmest of friends, __________ people also spend a large amount of time alone because they like solitude.

self-actualized p. 365

According to Maslow, people with a high need for privacy are not necessarily trying to __________ from relationships.

escape p. 365

For some people, _________ of solitude can provide the opportunity to develop spiritually and creatively.

long periods p. 368

Whether a person dislikes or enjoys time alone may be a function of _________ .

preference for solitude p. 368

Multiple Choice Questions

1. Advocates of the ___________ approach probably have generated less empirical research than psychologists from other approaches.

   a. biological
   b. behavioral/social learning
   c. humanistic
   d. trait

2. According to Jourard, making oneself "transparent" is the ultimate way for people to become

   a. more anxious.
   b. fully functioning.
   c. aware of the evaluations of others.
   d. all of the above

3. The dyadic effect is the observation that persons who disclose personal information in conversation tend to

   a. talk about others more than themselves.
   b. make judgments about the other person's self-esteem.
   c. match each other's level of intimacy.
   d. learn to distrust others quickly.

4. In a study of self-disclosure in which students took turns volunteering information about themselves, the students

   a. selected increasingly intimate topics.
   b. began with a discussion on trivial topics.
   c. tended to match their partners' level of intimacy.
   d. all of the above

5. Robert makes business trips to different cities once or twice a week and flies from airport to airport fairly frequently. Sometimes during long flights the passenger in the seat next to Robert engages him in a conversation. In these conversations between Robert and a perfect stranger, which is most likely?

   a. Any personal information that the stranger discloses will follow the many unstated social rules that govern conversations.
   b. The stranger will avoid making his or her specific opinions on social issues known.
   c. Robert will hear all kinds of personal information disclosed by the stranger.
   d. Robert will have to encourage the stranger for the conversation to move beyond trivial topics.

6. Which of the following is true about conversations among good friends?
    a. Noticeable signs of intimacy are lacking in conversations with strangers.
    b. Familiar terms are not used very often.
    c. There is little difference between the amount of self-disclosure with friends and with strangers.
    d. There is more confusion over when to speak than in conversations with strangers.

7. In a study in which participants read about someone who was either highly disclosing or not very disclosing, results showed that
    a. more participants thought the high discloser was a man.
    b. those who thought they were reading about a woman rated the person as better adjusted when she was disclosing.
    c. those who thought they were reading about a woman rated the person as better adjusted when she was not very disclosing.
    d. those who thought they were reading about a man rated the person as better adjusted when he was disclosing.

8. Self-disclosing men are seen as well adjusted as long as
    a. they talk about very intimate events.
    b. they talk about feminine topics.
    c. they do not self-disclose too much.
    d. they talk about masculine topics.

9. Men and women are more likely to be accepted when they disclose according to appropriate gender roles in society. For men, this means
    a. withholding information for the most part.
    b. disclosing information that is misleading or simply false.
    c. never revealing anything about one's self.
    d. none of the above

10. Jenny participated in a research study for credit in her college psychology class. She was asked to write about an experience that was personally upsetting for fifteen minutes every night for several nights in a row. Six months later Jenny is contacted by the researchers. Assuming Jenny is relatively healthy, which do you expect?
    a. Jenny visits the college health center more often than before.
    b. Jenny talks about trivial topics to her friends since the study six months ago.
    c. There is no change in the average number of days Jenny misses class due to illness.
    d. The average number of visits Jenny makes to the health center has dramatically declined.

11. Your best friend has been in an automobile accident in which others received serious injuries. According to research on disclosure of traumatic experiences, you suggest that your friend

    a. attempt to shut out any thoughts and feelings associated with the accident.
    b. talk about his or her feelings with friends or a trained therapist.
    c. avoid talking about the accident until it seems right to do so.
    d. write down any dreams he or she has for a month.

12. Some psychologists believe that feelings of loneliness reflect a deeper concern about existential questions of

    a. the existence of a supreme being.
    b. alienation.
    c. the search for meaning in one's life.
    d. both b and c

13. Psychologists in which of the following approaches to personality have shown the most interest in the topic of human loneliness besides humanistic psychologists?

    a. the biological approach
    b. the trait approach
    c. the behavioral/social learning approach
    d. the psychoanalytic approach

14. Correlational research has revealed that lonely people tend to

    a. have difficulty adjusting to new experiences.
    b. feel comfortable when others open up to them.
    c. have difficulty making new friends.
    d. all of the above

15. According to humanistic psychologists, one reason some people are chronically lonely is that they

    a. avoid social contact out of fear.
    b. have a low need for Affiliation.
    c. fear a loss of control associated with social interaction and relationships.
    d. have low or negative expectations of themselves.

16. Diego is a lonely college student who has been given a group assignment for which he must evaluate his own performance and the performance of three other students in his group. It is likely that Diego's evaluation of his own performance is

    a. lower than his evaluation of the other members of the group.
    b. higher than his evaluation of the other members of the group.
    c. similar to his evaluation of the other members of the group.
    d. left incomplete or not handed in to the instructor.

17. Very few people feel entirely good or bad about themselves, but typically these feelings are in regard to

    a. specific domains.
    b. academic performance.
    c. one's ego ideal.
    d. global self-esteem.

18. People low in self-esteem typically react to failure by

    a. losing their motivation.
    b. looking for excuses to which they can attribute their failure.
    c. making negative assessments of others.
    d. seeking psychotherapy.

19. When high self-esteem people are confronted with a negative evaluation, they

    a. easily blame others for the results.
    b. tell themselves how well they do in other areas.
    c. distort the outcome or deny the evaluation.
    d. begin to self-disclose at higher rates.

20. Lenny is anxious about his statistics assignment and so he waits until a high demand day in the computer lab to work on his assignment. He uses the lack of availability of computers as an excuse for not completing the assignment. For the next assignment he finds a computer for which the printer is not working properly. Lenny's behavior illustrates the self-protection motive called

    a. passive-aggressive.
    b. self-handicapping.
    c. self-abasement.
    d. self-affirmation.

21. In one study researchers compared the average self-esteem scores for Asian people as a function of their exposure to North American culture. Results showed that the most similar levels of self-esteem were obtained for

    a. recent immigrants, long-term immigrants, and Asians who had been abroad.
    b. long-term immigrants, second-generation, and third-generation Asian-Canadians.
    c. recent immigrants, Asians who had been abroad, and Asians who had never been abroad before.
    d. recent immigrants, long-term immigrants, and second-generation Asian-Canadians.

22. In order to measure self-esteem stability, researchers have

    a. asked people to self-disclose.
    b. looked at how people respond to positive and negative feedback.
    c. asked people to regularly report their feelings of self-worth.
    d. all of the above

23. Results of research on time spent alone confirms the hypothesis that

    a. monks and other people who live in seclusion are more likely to be introverts.
    b. Americans spend a significant amount of time in solitude.
    c. solitude becomes a less common experience with age.
    d. Americans tend to be more socially anxious than members of other cultures.

24. Several researchers have found that, for many people, isolation can have benefits. Studies have shown that solitude can be divided into different experiences based on

    a. the distance one keeps from other people.
    b. the length of time spent alone.
    c. the average number of people with whom one interacts.
    d. the goal or goals one has in mind for the period of solitude.

Integrative Questions

1. Specify the several benefits to clients of psychotherapy from self-disclosing interactions. Give an example of disclosure reciprocity and discuss the circumstances and rules under which people self-disclose. (340-348)

2. List the gender differences found in research on self-disclosure. Give one possible reason for each difference on your list. (343-344)

3. State four reasons why psychologists have shown a concern with loneliness. What other psychologists outside the humanistic approach have been concerned with loneliness and what was their specific interest in it? (348-349)

4. How is loneliness defined and measured? Given your understanding of psychoanalytic psychology, how do you suppose Sullivan or Fromm would go about studying loneliness? (349-350, 121-130)

5. Discuss the specific research findings on self-esteem and failure. Point out any contradictory evidence for the differences between people who are low and people who are high in self-esteem. Explain differences in reactions to failures. (355-358)

6. Discuss how high self-esteem and low self-esteem persons differ in their motives. Given these differences, what would you say is the prospect for stability in self-esteem between these personalities? (359-361)

7. How do people react to time alone? What factors determine whether an individual prefers solitude? Are there any benefits to spending time alone? If so, what are they? (365-369)

Evaluative Questions

1. Is it true that only through self-disclosure can we truly come to know ourselves? From your understanding of self-disclosure and its benefits, give evidence from your own experience that self-disclosure facilitates self-awareness. (339, 344-348)

2. Why do we reciprocate disclosure of intimacy, according to Jourard? Are there other reasons for this behavior? Critically evaluate these reasons and give your own analysis of disclosure reciprocity. (342-343)

3. Consider someone you know who seems lonely. What characteristics of lonely people are displayed in the person you are thinking about? State two ways in which you can help the person overcome feelings of loneliness. (348-354)

4. Evaluate the differences in self-esteem for different cultures. What makes them different in this respect? For what purpose do we take questions and concepts of personality, like self-esteem, to other cultures for study? (362-364)

5. Given that research indicates that interpersonal relationships are among the most important sources of happiness, why should some people desire their privacy? Give an answer to this question from the biological, trait, psychoanalytic, and humanistic approaches to personality. With which do you agree most? Support your answer. (365)

Answers to Multiple Choice Questions

1.	c, 337	9.	a, 344	17.	a, 355
2.	b, 339	10.	c, 345	18.	a, 356
3.	c, 341	11.	b, 348	19.	b, 358
4.	d, 341	12.	d, 349	20.	b, 360
5.	c, 342	13.	d, 349	21.	d, 363
6.	a, 343	14.	c, 351	22.	c, 360
7.	b, 343	15.	d, 351	23.	b, 366
8.	d, 344	16.	a, 351	24.	b, 368

Chapter 13

The Behavioral/Social Learning Approach

Theory, Application, and Assessment

Behaviorism

Basic Principles of Conditioning

Social Learning Theory

Social-Cognitive Theory

Application: Behavior Modification and Self-Efficacy Therapy

Assessment: Behavior Observation Methods

Strengths and Criticisms of the Behavioral/Social Learning Approach

Learning Objectives

1. Define behaviorism. Describe John B. Watson's reasons for advocating that the subject matter of psychology should be overt behavior.
2. State Watson's definition of personality in your own words. Give the names and research findings of two scientists who influenced Watson.
3. Contrast the radical behaviorism of Skinner with the behaviorism of Watson. Explain what Skinner has said about personal freedom and dignity.
4. Describe the process of classical conditioning with your own example. Include the key components UCS, UCR, CS, and CR in your example and use it to illustrate second-order conditioning. Define extinction and present the limitations of classical conditioning.

5. State the law of effect and describe the nature of the observations made by Thorndike to formulate the law.

6. Define operant conditioning. Contrast operant conditioning and classical conditioning. Illustrate with your own examples two reinforcement strategies used in operant conditioning to increase desired behaviors.

7. Discuss how extinction and punishment are each used to decrease unwanted behaviors. Discuss the several limitations of each of these methods.

8. Give your own example of shaping. State the circumstances under which shaping is particularly useful. Define generalization and discrimination and give examples of two personality characteristics that could be explained by these processes.

9. Discuss the origins of social learning theory and explain how it expands upon the behavioral approach to personality.

10. List the basic tenets of Rotter's theory and discuss the relationships among behavior potential, expectancy, and reinforcement value. Explain how different personality characteristics are related to differences in locus of control and reinforcement value.

11. Name the basic tenets of Bandura's social-cognitive theory and compare the theory with the strict behaviorist approach. Describe the reciprocal determinism model and discuss how the three parts of the model interact.

12. Define self-regulation and give examples of behavior that can be explained in the absence of external reinforcements and punishments.

13. Define observational learning and distinguish between learning and performance. Explain where our expectations come from for behaviors we have never performed before. Describe Bandura's experiment with nursery school children that investigated television and aggression.

14. Discuss how classical or operant conditioning could explain psychological disorders such as paranoia, aggression, and phobias. Describe how Watson used classical conditioning to create fear in a baby and how one might use classical conditioning to reduce such fear.

15. Define behavior modification. State the basic operant conditioning procedures typically used to change problem behaviors in individuals and in groups.

16. Define self-efficacy and distinguish between outcome expectations and efficacy expectations. State why self-efficacy falls within the domain of social learning theory and list the four sources of efficacy expectations.

17. State three purposes of objective behavioral assessment. Summarize the principles of direct observation procedures.

18. Define self-monitoring and state why it may be used as an alternative to direct observation. Describe the typical procedures used in self-monitoring and the disadvantages associated with its use. Give reasons for the use of observation by others as a method of behavior assessment.

19. Give the strengths of the behavioral/social learning approach to personality that has made it withstand the test of time. Discuss the advantages behavior modification procedures have over other therapy approaches.

20. State the limitations of the behavioral/social learning approach to personality. Distinguish among the criticisms given by humanistic psychologists and those of the biological approach to personality.

Important Concepts

radical behaviorism (p. 375)
unconditioned stimulus (p. 378)
unconditioned response (p. 378)
conditioned stimulus (p. 378)
conditioned response (p. 378)
second-order conditioning (p. 378)
extinction (p. 379)
law of effect (p. 379)
positive reinforcement (p. 380)
negative reinforcement (p. 380)
shaping (p. 382)
generalization (p. 382)
discrimination (p. 382)
social learning theory (p. 383)
social-cognitive theory (p. 383, 388)
reinforcement value (p. 384, 387)
expectancy (p. 384)
behavior potential (p. 384)
behavior-environment-behavior interactions (p. 383)
locus of control (p. 386)
generalized expectancies (p. 386)
reciprocal determinism (p. 388)
potential environment (p. 389)
actual environment (p. 389)
self-regulation (p. 390)
learning vs. performance (p. 391)
systematic desensitization (p. 395)
token economy (p. 397)
outcome expectation (p. 397)
efficacy expectation (p. 397)
enactive mastery experiences (p. 398)
vicarious experiences (p. 398)
guided mastery (p. 399)
direct observation (p. 400)
self-monitoring (p. 402)
observation by others (p. 403)

InfoTrac *Search terms:*

behaviorism (p. 373)
classical conditioning (p. 377)
operant conditioning (p. 380)
reinforcement (p. 380)
punishment (p. 380)
observational learning (p. 391)
behavior modification (p. 395)
aversion therapy (p. 396)
biofeedback (p. 397)
self-efficacy (p. 397)
role-playing (p. 401)

Programmed Review

According to Watson, thinking was simply behavior he called "subvocal speech," evidenced by the movements of the ________ .

vocal cords p. 373

Behaviorists believe that ________ can be examined to understand the processes that shape our personalities.

conditioning principles p. 377

When an S-R association exists without conditioning, then the response in the association is called ________ .

an unconditioned response p. 377

The process of using one conditioned S-R association to condition another S-R association is called ________ .

second-order conditioning p. 378

When the consequence of a behavior increases the behavior's frequency, the consequence is referred to as ________ .

a reinforcement p. 380

Although it is the most efficient method of decreasing undesired behavior, _______ is often a problem because people reinforce the undesired behavior without knowing it.

extinction p. 381

Arthur Staats introduced the notion of "behavior-environment-behavior interactions" in his ________theory.

social learning p. 383

A basic tenet of Rotter's social learning theory is that the strength of ________ is determined by the expectancy and value we place on reinforcement.

behavior potential p. 384

Beliefs about whether or not our actions are likely to be reinforced or punished are called ________ .

generalized expectancies p. 386

Bandura said that some of the most important causes of behavior, like thinking and symbolic processing, are capacities that are ________ by strict behaviorists.

overlooked p. 388

When there are no immediate reinforcements or punishments in the environment, Bandura argues that our actions are controlled by ________ .

self-regulation p. 390

Many complex human behaviors cannot be learned through classical or operant conditioning but are acquired through ________ .

observational learning p. 391

Using the principles of behaviorism to change problem behaviors is generally referred to as ________.

behavior modification p. 395

________ is a treatment for problem behavior that uses classical conditioning to associate undesired responses with aversive images.

Aversion therapy p. 396

The behavior therapy called ________ requires special equipment that provides information about somatic processes such as muscle tension and heart rate.

biofeedback p. 397

According to self-efficacy theory, how long people persist in their efforts to change their behavior is determined by ________ .

efficacy expectations p. 397

Using the procedure of ________ , a therapist arranges a situation so that a successful experience for the client is virtually guaranteed.

guided mastery p. 399

In the method of behavioral assessment known as _________, sometimes therapists ask clients to role-play.

direct observation p. 400

A benefit of the _________ method of behavior assessment is that clients are forced to pay attention to their problem behavior.

self-monitoring p. 402

One reason for the relatively long duration of the behavioral/social learning approach to personality is its solid foundation in ___________.

empirical research p. 404

Multiple Choice Questions

1. Watson argued that if psychology were to be a science, then psychologists must discontinue examining

   a. mental states.
   b. the unconscious.
   c. personality traits.
   d. brain functions.

2. According to the behavioral approach, personality is

   a. the result of inherited predispositions to behave in certain ways.
   b. a function of how we feel about conditions in the environment.
   c. the combination of environmental circumstances and unconscious impulses.
   d. the consistent patterns of behavior we engage in.

3. According to Watson, personality is

   a. the result of classical and operant conditioning.
   b. determined by both the environment and our own biology.
   c. a pattern of behavior resulting from our inner thoughts and experiences.
   d. the end product of our habit systems.

4. The process used in Pavlov's famous demonstrations of learning became known to the scientific community as

   a. classical conditioning.
   b. operant conditioning.
   c. instrumental conditioning.
   d. behaviorism.

5. According to Skinner, when a person says they are talkative because they are happy, then

   a. happiness is the cause of the person's talkativeness.
   b. the person has only put a label on their talkativeness.
   c. the person has given an explanation of their talkativeness.
   d. talkativeness is the real cause of the person's happiness.

6. Leticia is allergic to flowers and when she comes near a flower she starts to sneeze. She even sneezes when she is near artificial flowers. In terms of classical conditioning, artificial flowers are

   a. an unconditioned response to her allergy.
   b. an unconditioned stimulus for sneezing.
   c. a conditioned stimulus for sneezing.
   d. an unconditioned stimulus for her allergy.

7. From his observations of cats escaping from a "puzzle box" to obtain a piece of fish, Thorndike developed a theory that is known as

   a. the law of operant conditioning.
   b. the law of effect.
   c. the law of consequences.
   d. the law of association.

8. George is stopped by a police officer after running a red light. After checking on George's driving record, the officer suspends his driving privileges. The officer is using _________ to modify George's behavior.

   a. positive reinforcement
   b. negative reinforcement
   c. punishment
   d. extinction

9. A baseball trainer works with a player to improve his hitting with successive attempts to produce more hits each week of the season. The trainer is using

   a. stimulus generalization.
   b. discrimination.
   c. punishment.
   d. shaping.

10. Responding differently to rewarded and unrewarded stimuli is called

   a. generalization.
   b. domain specificity.
   c. discrimination.
   d. self-regulation.

11. Social learning theory developed out of behaviorism when many psychologists began to question

   a. whether the scope of behaviorism's subject matter was too limited.
   b. the usefulness of classical conditioning.
   c. the study of mental concepts.
   d. the assertion that operant conditioning is based on consequences.

12. According to Rotter, which of the following are psychological variables that must be considered to account for behavior?

   a. beliefs
   b. perceptions
   c. estimations of likelihoods
   d. all of the above

13. With respect to the locus of control continuum, Sally has an external orientation. Which of the following statements would she *least* likely make?

   a. "Hard work and perseverance pays off."
   b. "If my luck doesn't change, then I'll never get married."
   c. "I failed my psychology final because the professor doesn't like me."
   d. "If I die in a car crash, then it was my time."

14. In addition to external causes of behavior, Bandura argued that there are internal determinants as well. Which of the following is *not* an internal influence?

   a. experiences
   b. beliefs
   c. thoughts
   d. expectancies

15. From Bandura's research on observational learning in children we can conclude that whether a child performs an aggressive act depends on

    a. the amount of social encouragement the child has received to be aggressive.
    b. how extremely aggressive the behavior is.
    c. whether the model's behavior is reinforced or punished.
    d. whether the model is the child's parent.

16. The conditioned stimulus (CS) and unconditioned stimulus (UCS) in Watson and Rayner's experiment with a baby known as Little Albert were

    a. a white rat and a slap on the wrist.
    b. a loud noise and crying.
    c. fear responses and a loud noise.
    d. a white rat and a loud noise.

17. A treatment technique used to cure phobias by pairing images of the feared object with a relaxation response is called

    a. aversion therapy.
    b. aggression therapy.
    c. biofeedback.
    d. systematic desensitization.

18. According to the textbook, which of the following treatments for problem behaviors is an application of operant conditioning?

    a. aversion therapy
    b. biofeedback
    c. systematic desensitization
    d. all of the above

19. One of the assumptions of self-efficacy theory is that there is a difference between believing that something can happen and believing that you can make it happen. The extent of people's beliefs that they can bring about outcomes is referred to as

    a. reinforcement value.
    b. efficacy expectation.
    c. outcome expectation.
    d. performance accomplishments.

20. Jill watches her roommate Melissa study every evening for two hours before watching television. She is aware that Melissa really doesn't mind studying once she has started and even seems to enjoy it. Jill forms an efficacy expectation that she also can study each night for a period of time based on

    a. vicarious experience.
    b. verbal persuasion.
    c. emotional arousal.
    d. none of the above

21. In their practice of psychotherapy, behavior therapists

    a. spend a great deal of effort uncovering the true cause of the client's problem.
    b. see overt behaviors as a sign of an underlying psychological problem.
    c. focus on observable behaviors without much reference to the underlying cause of the problem.
    d. attempt to determine the biological basis of some behaviors.

22. One problem with the self-monitoring method is that

    a. it cannot be used to assess the progress of treatment.
    b. the client may be dishonest about their behavior.
    c. the client is not a trained psychotherapist.
    d. it may be contaminated by self-report measures.

23. Which of the following is *not* a strength of the behavioral/social learning approach?

    a. the breadth of its description of human personality
    b. its solid foundation in empirical research
    c. the usefulness of the therapeutic procedures based on it
    d. the duration of behavior therapy compared to other approaches

24. A criticism of the behavioral/social learning approach to personality is that

    a. behaviorists rejected free will as a determinant of behavior.
    b. the role of heredity is not given adequate attention.
    c. behavior therapists distort the real therapy issues in their narrow focus.
    d. all of the above

Integrative Questions

1. Why can it be said that Skinner's views of human behavior are like Freud's? (376)

2. List specific ways in which social learning theory provides a bridge between traditional behaviorism and the more recent cognitive approaches to personality. (383-384)

3. On what grounds can it be said that the behavioral/social learning theory approach to personality is similar to the trait approach? In what ways are these approaches distinct? (388-391)

4. Contrast behavioral and social-cognitive explanations for why siblings growing up in the same home environment develop different personalities. How do these explanations differ from purely biological explanations of personality? (391-393)

5. Bandura has said that behavior modification does not change people as much as it provides a method for people to change if they believe they can. On what assumptions is Bandura's idea based? Would a psychoanalyst or a humanist agree and why? (397-399)

6. State the reasons for each of the procedures involved in direct behavior observation. How do these methods differ from assessment methods used in psychoanalysis? (400-402, 57)

7. How might a behavior therapist use direct observation and self-monitoring to determine an appropriate treatment for undesired behavior? Give your own example of a problem behavior and how to use these methods to achieve reliable assessments of the problem. What would take place in each method? (400-403)

8. What were the basic empirical research findings of Watson, Skinner, Rotter, and Bandura? Give at least one unique contribution that each made to the behavioral/social learning approach to personality. (373-377, 383-387)

9. Contrast the following approaches to therapy in terms of the relative amount of time the treatment is expected to last: psychoanalytic, behavioral, and biological. (395)

Evaluative Questions

1. What do you think of Watson's famous statement, "Give me a dozen healthy infants, well formed, and my own specified world to bring them up in, and I'll guarantee to take any one at random and train him to become any type of specialist I might select"? Give evidence from your understanding of personality to explain why you agree or disagree. (375)

2. Most people understand that there is a connection between actions and consequences in shaping behavior. Since most people routinely rely on this understanding to shape other people's behavior, what is the justification of so much research on operant conditioning principles? (377-383)

3. If you were a behavior therapist seeking to change the problem behaviors of a teenager, would you choose reinforcement or punishment? Why? (381)

4. As you know there are a number of differences between radical behaviorism and social learning theory. Can social learning theory predict behavior better than the behavioral approach? If so, name several kinds of behaviors for which expectancy is a better predictor than experience. (383-387)

5. State the usefulness of self-efficacy therapy by discussing its advantages over behavior modification in explaining behavior problems. Speculate on the limitations of self-efficacy theory by giving an example of a behavior problem for which efficacy expectations have little impact. (395-399)

6. Discuss the advantages and disadvantages of each of the methods of behavior assessment in the behavioral/social learning approach. If you were a behavior therapist attempting to assess and treat a case of strong fear in a three-year-old child, which method of behavior assessment would you use and why? (400-403)

7. Suppose you were a behavior therapist who adhered to social learning theory. A client is presented to you who suffers from symptoms of schizophrenia. Assuming there is a biological predisposition underlying the disorder, what are the relative advantages and disadvantages of using behavior modification procedures to help the person? (403-407)

Answers to Multiple Choice Questions

1.	a, 373	13.	c, 386
2.	d, 373	14.	a, 388
3.	d, 375	15.	c, 392
4.	a, 377	16.	d, 394
5.	b, 377	17.	d, 395
6.	c, 378	18.	b, 397
7.	b, 379	19.	b, 397
8.	c, 381	20.	a, 398
9.	d, 382	21.	c, 400
10.	c, 382	22.	b, 403
11.	a, 383	23.	a, 406
12.	d, 384	24.	d, 406

Chapter 14

The Behavioral/Social Learning Approach

Relevant Research

Individual Differences in Gender-Role Behavior

Observational Learning of Aggression

Learned Helplessness

Locus of Control

Learning Objectives

1. State why traditional animal research in scientific psychology is not outside of the human condition.
2. Define gender roles. Describe the general processes by which different gender-role behaviors are acquired. Define the masculinity-femininity construct and state the two assumptions upon which this early scale was based.
3. Define androgyny. Explain how the androgyny concept challenged the assumptions of the masculinity-femininity approach and in what ways it increased our understanding of gender roles.
4. Describe the characteristics of gender-role inventories. Distinguish among the four sex-type categories into which researchers can place people based on these scales.
5. Describe three models that attempt to explain the relationship between gender-type and psychological adjustment. Summarize the research findings for each of these models. Give three general conclusions that can be drawn from research about the effects of gender-type on psychological health.

6. Give examples of research findings that support a relationship between gender-type and interpersonal relations. State the gender characteristics of the ideal marriage partner and three reasons suggested by research for why such characteristics are preferred.
7. Describe Bandura's Four-Step Model. Explain why each step is necessary for people to imitate aggressive behavior and describe the circumstances under which people are more likely to imitate aggressive acts.
8. Discuss research findings on aggression in the media that lead psychologists to believe that viewing aggression increases the likelihood of acting aggressively.
9. Define learned helplessness. Describe the classical conditioning research that led to the concept and state how the animals inappropriately generalized their learning.
10. Describe one research method used to test learned helplessness in humans. Specify the application of learned helplessness to two human problems and the solutions that research has suggested for each.
11. Define locus of control. Distinguish between internal and external locus of control and discuss the relationship between locus of control and well-being. Include evidence with regard to achievement and psychotherapy.
12. Explain how one's physical health can be predicted by one's position along the locus of control dimension.

Important Concepts

gender-role socialization (p. 411)
masculinity-femininity (p. 412)
agency (p. 414)
communion (p. 414)
undifferentiated (p. 414)
congruence model (p. 415)
androgyny model (p. 415)
masculinity model (p. 416)
Bem Sex Role Inventory (p. 417)
unmitigated agency (p. 419)
unmitigated communion (p. 419)
Four-Step Model (p. 420)
serotonin (p. 433)
generalized expectancies (p. 434)
external locus of control (p. 434)
internal locus of control (p. 434)

InfoTrac *Search terms:*

gender roles (p. 412)
androgyny (p. 413)
learned helplessness (p. 428)
locus of control (p. 434)

Programmed Review

Behaviorists and social learning theorists maintain gender differences are the result of a lifelong process called __________ .

gender-role socialization p. 411

Before the school years, children become aware of gender-role _________ mostly through their parents and peers.

expectations p. 412

In addition to operant conditioning, it is clear that gender-role behaviors are acquired through _________ .

observational learning p. 412

The fact that most people do not act in gender-appropriate ways illustrates that there are large _________ in the gender-role socialization of people.

individual differences p. 412

The _________ model is the least-supported explanation for how gender-type affects psychological adjustment.

congruence p. 415

When people form first impressions of others, _________ is the gender-type liked by most people.

androgynous p. 416

According to research, being married to someone who lacks feminine characteristics is indicative of _________ marriage.

an unhappy p. 419

To learn aggressive behavior through observation, people must not only attend to a model's behavior but also must _________ the behavior.

remember p. 421

Evidence shows that the average American child will view about _______ murders on television before leaving elementary school.

8,000 p. 423

In the first demonstrations of learned helplessness dogs were subjected to _________ .

electric shocks p. 428

Learned helplessness in the elderly often takes the form of a lack of ________ .

motivation and activity p. 431

Depressed persons often lack the ________ to even get out of bed in the morning.

motivation p. 432

Much data suggest that exposure to ________ events can be a cause of depression.

uncontrollable p. 433

Research on locus of control was developed out of Rotter's concept of ________ .

generalized expectancies p. 434

A recent study found that HIV-positive men with an external locus of control were ________ about their condition than those with an internal locus of control.

more depressed p. 436

Internals seem to do better in school because they see themselves as ________ .

responsible p. 438

Several studies have shown that ________ are healthier and practice better health habits.

internals p. 440

Multiple Choice Questions

1. With which of the following concepts is Rotter associated?
   a. learned helplessness
   b. observational learning of aggression
   c. classical conditioning
   d. locus of control

2. By which of the following processes does gender-role socialization take place?
   a. classical conditioning
   b. operant conditioning
   c. biological sex differentiation
   d. all of the above

3. Sarah has the flexibility to engage in masculine behaviors when the situation dictates, but she is sex-typed as both masculine and feminine. Which of the following is likely to be true about Sarah?

   a. She will be more well adjusted than her more feminine-typed friends.
   b. She will disengage from androgyny as she develops.
   c. She is best classified as undifferentiated.
   d. Sarah's personality tends toward agency and away from communion.

4. Under which of the following categories would a person fall who scores low on both masculine and feminine scales of a gender-role inventory?

   a. androgynous
   b. masculine
   c. feminine
   d. undifferentiated

5. Sam and Sally are in a debate about gender roles. Sam says, "I think men should be masculine and women should be feminine." Sally disagrees and argues that the most well adjusted people in society have the ability to respond with feminine or masculine behaviors depending on the situation. Sally agrees with which model?

   a. congruence model
   b. androgyny model
   c. masculinity model
   d. femininity model

6. Which of the following inventories is among the more popular ones for gender-role research?

   a. Bem Sex Role Inventory
   b. Minnesota Multiphasic Personality Inventory
   c. Rotter Androgyny Scale
   d. both a and b

7. All but which of the following statements is a reason why the most preferable partners in romantic relationships are feminine or androgynous people?

   a. Their behavior emphasizes control and self-restraint.
   b. They are better at expressing romantic feelings.
   c. They are easy to talk to.
   d. They have greater ability to resolve disputes.

8. According to Bandura, if a person pays attention to a model's aggressive act and its consequences, and the person has the ability to enact what they have seen, then

    a. it is highly probable that the person will engage in the act.
    b. the person must also be able to remember the act to imitate it.
    c. outcome expectations matter little.
    d. performance has taken place but not learning.

9. Controlled laboratory research on observational learning of aggression requires participants to watch a violent or nonviolent program and then

    a. receive the opportunity to act aggressively.
    b. complete a questionnaire about their experience.
    c. engage in a group discussion of the program.
    d. take a test on their memory for details of the program.

10. Investigators who measured how much television was watched by a group of eight-year-old children found that twenty-two years later, at age thirty, children who had watched high amounts of television

    a. were more chronically depressed as adults.
    b. were more likely to have been convicted for crimes as adults.
    c. were less likely to engage in serious crimes as adults.
    d. did not appreciate the impact of violent television on their own children.

11. Dogs exposed to aversive stimuli from which they could not escape were found to

    a. learn through observation how to be helpless.
    b. avoid the stimulus on every trial.
    c. stop moving when placed in a shuttle-box situation.
    d. suffer from neurological damage.

12. Which of the following are ways in which humans can learn to be helpless?

    a. by being told they are helpless
    b. by observational learning
    c. by classical conditioning
    d. all of the above

13. Animals exposed to inescapable shock and depressed humans are similar in that both

    a. show evidence for internal locus of control.
    b. continue to try to escape adversity until exhaustion.
    c. become highly agitated and aggressive.
    d. have similar changes in neurotransmitters and receptors.

14. Willy is a teenager who thinks that his swimming medals are the result of his effort. Mindy believes that her batting average in softball is the result of luck. Rotter would say that Willy has an ________ locus of control orientation and Mindy has a(n) ________ locus of control orientation.

    a. internal; external
    b. external; internal
    c. internal; generalized
    d. external; superstitious

15. In a study of suicidal patients, when asked to relive the events that took place before an attempted suicide, the patients

    a. experienced terrifying flashbacks.
    b. described themselves in terms of an internal locus of control.
    c. described themselves in terms of an external locus of control.
    d. had no memory because the events had been repressed.

16. Studies of achievement have shown that external students

    a. perform better on academic tests than internals in elementary school.
    b. get better grades than internals in college.
    c. receive lower scores on achievement tests in high school.
    d. all of the above

17. Which of the following is true about a therapy client's locus of control orientation?

    a. Externals become less depressed when their spouse provides support.
    b. The most effective therapy happens when procedures match the client's orientation.
    c. Internals show the most improvement when they could give their own rewards.
    d. all of the above

18. People with an internal locus of control may be more healthy than people with an external locus of control because

    a. internals do not concern themselves with the nature of illnesses.
    b. externals consume less healthy food and possess poor eating habits.
    c. internals tend to perform more preventative behaviors.
    d. externals cooperate with physicians more than internals.

Integrative Questions

1. Now that you have studied the chapter, make a list of as many social problems or personal lifestyle issues that you can remember from the textbook. For each issue, give the general research finding that can be applied toward its solution. (409-441)

2. In what ways do stimulus generalization and discrimination contribute to the acquisition of gender-role behavior? Give an example of your own to illustrate your answer. (382, 411-412)

3. There are three explanations given in the textbook for how gender-type might affect psychological adjustment. What are these explanations and the research evidence supporting them? Are all three equally supported? (415-417)

4. Describe the relationship between frustration and aggression in children. How does the behavioral/social learning explanation differ from that of neo-Freudian theory? (421-423, 147)

5. In what way does outcome expectancy play a role in Bandura's Four-Step Model? Give an example of an aggressive act that can be attended to, remembered, and enacted but fails to have reinforcement value. (384, 420-423)

6. Draw a matrix that contrasts models of depression from the psychoanalytic, humanistic, and behavioral approaches. Place the perspectives along the columns. Make the first row the assessment techniques for each perspective and make the second row descriptions of treatment applications for people with depression. (59-63, 324-325, 328, 432-434)

7. Discuss the relationship between the constructs called learned helplessness and locus of control. Consider the research findings on elderly and depressed populations and state what aspects of these people's personality fit both constructs. (428-438)

8. Therapists from the humanistic perspective believe clients seeking help should be given complete control over the therapy. Based on the concept of locus of control, would a social learning theorist agree with this approach to treatment? Why or why not? (324, 439)

9. What role does Rotter's concept of generalized expectancies play in locus of control and physical health? Which group is more likely to have high efficacy expectations about their health, internals or externals? In contrast, how would a radical behaviorist explain the relationship between locus of control and health? (384-387, 440-441)

Evaluative Questions

1. Think of your many friends and acquaintances. Describe the behavior of two people you know, one male and one female, who seem to cross traditional gender roles. Include examples of their behavior that illustrate this reversal. Is it fair to say that in today's world with less gender restrictions there is little reason to conduct research on gender roles? (412-419)

2. Some researchers believe that the characteristics underlying masculinity and femininity should be the focus of research rather than the traits themselves. Do you agree? Why or why not? Given what you know about gender-role research, in what ways might such a change in focus contribute to our understanding of gender-role behavior? (414-419)

3. Suppose a friend tells you that the happiest couples are those with one masculine member and one feminine member because these are complementary traits. Based on the research evidence, would you agree? Is the belief held by your friend true for short-term relationships or long-term ones? (417-419)

4. Now that you are familiar with the relevant research on observational learning of aggression, do you think it is likely that John Hinckley learned to try to assassinate President Reagan from repeatedly watching the movie *Taxi Driver*? For the Hinckley case, consider the likelihood of each step in the Four-Step Model and give research evidence to support your estimate. (420, 423-428)

5. Can it be said with some certainty that viewing aggression increases the likelihood of acting aggressively? For each research finding in support of this assertion state one alternative explanation for the evidence. Would you consider selling your television? (423-428)

6. Learned helplessness has been explained by behaviorists that humans, like dogs, incorrectly generalize their helplessness to situations that they could control. How might this explanation for human learned helplessness differ from the perspective of a social learning theorist like Bandura? Why can it be said that it is often better to let the elderly take care of themselves? (429-432)

7. How might an organizational psychologist apply the locus of control concept to increase productivity and job satisfaction? Give your own example of a job task in which this application could work. (327, 434, 438)

8. If your mother told you that psychological disorders and health problems are caused by what people expect will happen, how might you respond? Would you say that health problems are caused more by external expectations or by reinforcement value? (436-438, 440-441)

Answers to Multiple Choice Questions

1. d, 410
2. b, 411
3. a, 414
4. d, 414
5. b, 415
6. d, 417
7. a, 419
8. b, 420
9. a, 425
10. b, 425
11. c, 428
12. d, 431
13. d, 433
14. a, 434
15. c, 437
16. c, 438
17. d, 439
18. c, 441

Chapter 15

The Cognitive Approach

Theory, Application, and Assessment

George Kelly's Personal Construct Theory

Cognitive Personality Variables

Cognitive Representations of the Self

Application: Cognitive Psychotherapy

Assessment: The Repertory Grid Technique

Strengths and Criticisms of the Cognitive Approach

Learning Objectives

1. Describe the development of the cognitive approach to personality and discuss an early predecessor from within the behavioral approach.
2. Discuss the fundamental ideas underlying Kelly's personal construct theory and describe the way in which the theory was structured. Explain the motivations behind behavior according to Kelly.
3. Define the concept of the personal construct and what is meant by range of convenience. Give two reasons why one person's personality is different from another's, according to Kelly's personal construct theory, and present his direct challenge to behavior theory.
4. Discuss the application of personal construct theory to psychological problems such as anxiety. Give two reasons why our constructs sometimes fail us. State why construct systems may be incomplete.
5. Narrate the development of research on cognitive personality variables. Define Mischel's cognitive-affective units and discuss individual differences in terms of these units.

6. Define schemas and give an example. Explain how this cognitive structure allows both stability and individual differences in personality.
7. Define prototypes and give an example. Describe the various functions of the prototype as a cognitive structure in personality.
8. Discuss the nature of the self-schema and explain how psychologists study hypothetical constructs like self-schemas. Explain what is meant by "possible selves" and discuss two functions of possible selves as cognitive structures.
9. Explain the importance of cognitive restructuring in therapy based on the cognitive approach. Describe the procedure called fixed-role therapy. Specify the elements of fixed-role therapy that make it a type of cognitive psychotherapy. Discuss the therapist's role in this kind of therapy.
10. Discuss Albert Ellis's rational-emotive therapy and highlight two goals of this cognitive approach to psychotherapy. Explain what is meant by the A-B-C process.
11. Describe the process of self-instructional training and identify its purpose. Indicate how it is similar to rational-emotive therapy.
12. Give the full name of the Rep test and explain its origin. Describe how the Rep test is used as a means of personality assessment and distinguish among various forms of the test.
13. Give three strengths of the cognitive approach to personality. State how the cognitive approach improves on other approaches to personality.
14. State three criticisms or weaknesses that have been made of the cognitive approach to personality. Explain why some argue there is no need to introduce cognitive concepts in personality theory.

Important Concepts

man-the-scientist (p. 444)
Fundamental Postulate (p. 446)
accessibility (p. 450)
cognitive-affective units (p. 450)
schemas (p. 451)
aschematic (p. 455)
possible selves (p. 457)
personifications (p. 458)
self-discrepancy theory (p. 458)
fixed-role therapy (p. 460)
Activating experience (p. 460)
irrational Belief (p. 460)
emotional Consequence (p. 460)
cognitive restructuring (p. 460)
self-instructional training (p. 463)
internal monologues (p. 463)
Rep test (p. 464)

InfoTrac *Search terms:*

George Kelly (p. 444)
personal constructs (p. 445)
self-schema (p. 453)
Albert Ellis (p. 460)
rational-emotive therapy (p. 460)

Programmed Review

The cognitive approach to personality explains differences in personality as differences in the way people _________ .

process information p. 444

According to Kelly, people want to understand the world so that they can _________ what happens to them.

predict and control p. 444

Kelly presented his theory of personality in a highly _________ manner.

organized and structured p. 446

Kelly maintained that differences in personality result largely from differences in the way people _________ .

construe the world p. 446

Not only are there a limitless number of constructs we can use, the ways in which we can _________ these constructs are limitless as well.

organize p. 448

Kelly suggested that the better we understand another person's ________ , the better we will get along.

construct system p. 448

Kelly argued that _________ is at the heart of most psychological problems.

anxiety p. 449

Mischel has argued that the events we encounter interact with a complex system of _________.

cognitive-affective units p. 450

Psychologist William James once referred to what the world looks like to a baby as a "bussing, blooming _________ ."

confusion p. 451

_________ are hypothetical cognitive structures that help us perceive, organize, process, and utilize information.

Schemas p. 451

In addition to allowing for rapid processing of schema-relevant information, self-schemas provide a ________ for organizing relevant information.

framework p. 455

_________ represent our dreams and aspirations as well as our fears and anxieties.

Possible selves p. 457

One function of possible selves is to help us interpret the _________ of our behavior and the events in our lives.

meaning p. 458

The approach of _________ proposes three different representations of the self.

self-discrepancy theory p. 458

Increased attention to cognitive structures has been paralleled by a growing interest in cognitive approaches to __________ .

psychotherapy p. 459

George Kelly's goal as a therapist was to help his clients develop new _________ .

constructs p. 460

According to Ellis, people have psychological problems because of faulty reasoning based on _________ .

irrational beliefs p. 460

According to the cognitive approach to personality, one reason for recurrent problems is that some people typically engage in _________ thinking.

self-defeating p. 463

In self-instructional training, therapists help clients prepare _________ for each step of the stressful experience.

internal monologues p. 463

Like most applications of personality theory, cognitive psychotherapy may not work for everyone but has been shown to be more successful than behavior therapy for the treatment of _________.

depression p. 463

One assumption of the Rep test is that the constructs clients provide also apply to _________ in new situations.

new people p. 465

One strength of the cognitive approach is that it fits well with the current _________ , or mood of psychology.

Zeitgeist p. 467

Multiple Choice Questions

1. One of the earliest psychologists to propose a cognitive model of personality was
    a. Carl Jung.
    b. Albert Bandura.
    c. Kurt Lewin.
    d. Walter Mischel.

2. To obtain a sense of predictability, Kelly suggests that we engage in
    a. template matching.
    b. scientific discovery.
    c. theory construction.
    d. hypothesis testing.

3. Which of the following is true about Kelly's Fundamental Postulate?
    a. He supported the psychoanalytic notion that past conflicts determine one's future actions.
    b. He believed that external stimuli are the basic influences on our behavior.
    c. He suggested that past experiences lead to constructs that help us anticipate events.
    d. all of the above

4. Which of the following corollaries suggests that a person decides for himself that alternative through which he anticipates the greater possibility for extension and definition of his system?

   a. construction corollary
   b. choice corollary
   c. organization corollary
   d. range corollary

5. According to Kelly, when constructs fail us as we try to predict events,

   a. old constructs are selected out of the system.
   b. failure to consider new information increases one's ability to make better predictions.
   c. new constructs are constantly generated to replace the old ones.
   d. we seldom accept it.

6. Within personal construct theory, anxiety occurs when

   a. one's construct system does not match the ideal system.
   b. one's constructs fail to become impermeable.
   c. we cannot predict future events.
   d. it becomes impossible to modify one's construct system.

7. Which of the following is true about the cognitive processes that produce behavior?

   a. Behaviorists argued that the situation is processed in the "black box."
   b. The processing that takes place between situation and response is of little importance.
   c. Cognitive-affective units are equally accessible from memory.
   d. Cognitive theorists acknowledge that the situation often initiates behavior.

8. When participants in a study of cognitive structures answered questions about __________, they were more likely to remember the information in the question.

   a. their partner or spouse
   b. their mother
   c. themselves
   d. concrete objects

9. Jessica makes an appointment to speak with her professor about the last exam in the class. She is quite surprised to find that there are no books in her professor's office. Jessica's surprise most likely results from a violation of her professor's office

   a. construct.
   b. prototype.
   c. cognitive-affective unit.
   d. schema.

10. Your self-schema consists of those aspects of your behavior that are

a. unique to you and you alone.
b. most important to you.
c. similar to your parents and, by extension, your family.
d. innate.

11. Early psychologists used the method of discovering _________ to study hypothetical constructs like the self-schema.

a. how quickly people respond
b. personality structure
c. dream content
d. how accurately people think

12. In a study of processing information through the self-schema, participants were more likely to remember the information when

a. words had the ability to generate emotions.
b. the information was about participants themselves.
c. a self-referent question was difficult to answer.
d. participants had to generate a rhyme.

13. Results of research on the possible selves of juvenile delinquents indicates that

a. only a few had developed a possible self of criminal.
b. most had developed a possible self of rapist.
c. many had developed possible selves for goals like having a job and doing well in school.
d. more than one-third had developed a possible self of criminal.

14. Each kind of cognitive therapy identifies _________ as the cause of disorders.

a. early childhood experiences
b. a loss of the meaning of life and freedom
c. inappropriate behaviors
d. inappropriate thoughts

15. Which of the following is *not* among the methods used by Kelly in psychotherapy?

a. asking people to clearly define their personal constructs
b. asking people to describe their ideal self
c. asking people to provide examples of their personal constructs
d. forcing people to attend to their process of construing the world

16. Which of the following is an emotional Consequence?

    a. an invitation to go to the movies with a friend
    b. a feeling that a character in a movie could be real
    c. becoming frightened by a movie
    d. the thought that things that happen in movies happen to people

17. One of the goals of rational-emotive therapy is

    a. to let clients be themselves.
    b. to help clients identify their true and irrational selves.
    c. for clients to replace irrational beliefs with rational ones.
    d. for clients to identify their strategies of problem solving.

18. People can best prepare for and deal with potentially distressing situations through the cognitive therapy known as

    a. rational-emotive therapy.
    b. self-instructional training.
    c. fixed-role therapy.
    d. person-centered therapy.

19. Which of the following is true about self-instructional training?

    a. Its purpose is to replace self-defeating thoughts with more appropriate and positive ones.
    b. Through self-instructional training one modifies their own cognitive structures.
    c. It helps people overcome problems they are currently dealing with.
    d. both b and c

20. One of the goals of Kelly's Rep test is to obtain a visual map of how clients

    a. feel about their anxiety or distress.
    b. can control unconscious impulses.
    c. construe the world.
    d. organize their self-schema.

21. A strength of the cognitive approach is that it fits well with

    a. modern artificial intelligence research.
    b. the psychoanalytic perspective.
    c. the behavioral/social learning approach.
    d. current trends in the field of psychology.

22. In which of the following ways has the cognitive approach been criticized?

    a. It has not been supported by enough research.
    b. It is not needed to explain individual differences in behavior.
    c. It has not added much to earlier approaches to personality.
    d. It does not fit well with current trends in psychology.

Integrative Questions

1. Compare Kelly's conception of human personality with Freud's view. Discuss the factors that influence personality and any similarities between these two conceptions. According to Kelly, how do we make predictions about the world? (46, 444-449)

2. How can personal constructs be used to explain personality differences? Make a list of the eleven corollaries proposed by Kelly and state what each means to you. Discuss three personality phenomena that are explained by personal construct theory. (447-449)

3. Discuss what is meant by the "black box." Contrast the cognitive approach to personality with the behavioral/social learning approach in terms of the black box. In what ways does cognitive theory improve on earlier explanations of situational influences on behavior? (450, 383-388)

4. Discuss the relationship in two paragraphs between the notion of possible selves and Sullivan's concept of personifications. (122, 458-459)

5. Contrast cognitive psychotherapy with the approaches of Freud and Rogers. Use the methods of Kelly as an example of cognitive therapy in your discussion. (59, 324, 459-462)

6. Contrast Kelly's approach to psychotherapy and Ellis's approach. What differences are in the goals of each approach? What assumptions are similar for each approach? (459-462)

7. How do psychotherapists use the Rep test for clinical analysis? Describe the steps involved in the test and the manner in which the data are interpreted. In what ways is this assessment similar to projective tests? (464-466, 57)

Evaluative Questions

1. State in your own words Kelly's Fundamental Postulate. Critically evaluate the postulate based on your own experiences. In what ways were Kelly's conception of humankind unique? (444-448)

2. As suggested in the textbook, ask yourself what things you are interested in learning about people when you first meet them. Write down the first thoughts you have. Analyze your thoughts and interpret them as personal constructs. How do your constructs make your personality unique? (446-448)

3. Give examples of cognitive-affective units that you have. Describe an example of a schema you have. State your schemas for a friendly person, an athletic person, an intelligent person, and a nurturing person. In a paragraph give a brief description of your own possible self. (450-459)

4. If you could see your self-schema, what would it look like? Describe it in words or sketch it out like Figure 15.2 in the text. Give an example of a behavior that has become part of who you are. What concept in Allport's approach to personality is similar to the core of one's self-schema? (173, 452-457)

5. Think of a strong emotional event that you have experienced recently. According to Ellis's approach to psychotherapy, identify the A, B, and C elements in your experience. Is your B element on the list in Table 15.3 of the text? (460-462)

6. Why do some psychologists think of self-instructional training like an inoculation? Explain the goals of this type of therapy. State why psychologists believe this approach is promising. (462-464)

Answers to Multiple Choice Questions

1.	c, 444	12.	b, 456
2.	a, 444	13.	d, 458
3.	c, 446	14.	d, 459
4.	b, 447	15.	b, 460
5.	c, 449	16.	c, 460
6.	c, 449	17.	c, 461
7.	d, 450	18.	b, 463
8.	c, 456	19.	a, 463
9.	d, 451	20.	c, 464
10.	b, 453	21.	d, 467
11.	a, 456	22.	b, 468

Chapter 16

The Cognitive Approach

Relevant Research

Freudian Concepts Revisited: Transference and Repression

Gender Type and Gender Differences

Cognitions and Depression

Learning Objectives

1. Specify the attitude of contemporary psychology to Freud's theory. State how modern psychology explains the relevance of some of Freud's original ideas.
2. Review the concept of transference from the psychoanalytic approach. Discuss a cognitive formulation of transference and research evidence that supports it.
3. Review the concept of repression, the cornerstone of the psychoanalytic approach. Explain the phenomenon of repression from a modern cognitive orientation based on individual differences and give the research evidence in support of it.
4. Identify the characteristics of repressors in terms of their response to unpleasant feelings, emotionality, and access to memory. Define selective attention and discuss its possible role in these characteristic responses.
5. Summarize the several differences in personality between men and women discovered from cognitive research on gender-types.
6. Describe gender schema theory and define gender schema. Discuss the cognitive implications of being sex-typed or not and how researchers go about studying differences in gender schemas.
7. Summarize the continuing issues for personality research on gender schemas.

8. Discuss how men and women differ in the way they process self-relevant information. Present two lines of research that propose reasons for this difference and the implications for how men and women cognitively represent themselves and what they remember.
9. Explain how depressive thoughts are related to depressing feelings. Discuss the concept of a depressive schema and the research evidence employing self-schema techniques that support the existence of a depressive schema.
10. Summarize the results of processing information through a depressive schema. Discuss how these cognitive phenomena help in our understanding of depressed people.
11. Discuss the attributional model of learned helplessness. State why the animal model of learned helplessness was insufficient for understanding humans. Define hopelessness depression and contrast it with helplessness depression.
12. Define explanatory style and the kinds of information people rely on to explain the events in their lives. Indicate why explanatory style may play a large role in human personality and how the relationship between attribution and depression is moderated by culture.
13. Discuss evidence from research that suggests a link between depression and some attributional dimensions but not others. State which are predictive of behavior and which are not.

Important Concepts

projection (p. 472)
repression (p. 475)
gender schema theory (p. 480)
clustering (p. 480)
independent self-construals (p. 484)
interdependent self-construals (p. 484)
depressive cognitive triad (p. 487)
depressive schema (p. 488)
attributional model (p. 492)
stable attributions (p. 492)
unstable attributions (p. 492)
internal attributions (p. 492)
external attributions (p. 492)
global attributions (p. 493)
specific attributions (p. 493)

InfoTrac *Search terms:*

transference (p. 473)
selective attention (p. 478)
gender schema (p. 480)
depression (p. 487)
explanatory style (p. 494)

Programmed Review

One might say that a suspicious person, rather than engaging in projection, has activated his or her "untrustworthy behavior" ________ .

schema p. 472

During therapy, some of Freud's patients would transfer their feelings about ________ to the therapist.

significant others p. 473

When personality researchers use the term *repression* today, they usually refer to the way some people respond to ________ .

unpleasant information p. 475

When repressors sense threatening information, they tend to engage in a ________ process.

selective attention p. 478

One way to demonstrate gender schema differences is to look at ________ gender-related information is processed.

how quickly p. 481

While men and women do not differ in their general memory abilities, they often show differences in ________ they remember.

what p. 482

Men often develop ________ in that their self-conceptions are relatively unrelated to the conceptions they have of others.

independent self-construals p. 484

Psychologists increasingly are turning to ________ to understand depression.

cognitive approaches p. 487

Although some maintain that negative thoughts are a symptom of depression, the cognitive approach suggests that negative thoughts ________ depression.

cause p. 487

Most people have an unrealistically _________ outlook on life.

positive p. 488

Much of the evidence for depressive schemas comes from studies employing the __________ research techniques.

self-schema p. 488

People processing information through a depressive schema have greater _________ to depressing memories.

access p. 489

Because depressed people focus on the negative, overcoming depression is _________ .

very difficult p. 491

According to the attributional model of learned helplessness, the explanations people give for their _________ determine whether learned helplessness develops.

lack of control p. 492

Relatively stable patterns in the kinds of attributions people make are called one's _________ .

explanatory style p. 494

The relationship between attributions and helplessness may be affected by _________ .

culture p. 495

Multiple Choice Questions

1. Obtaining a complete understanding of human personality requires that
   a. we focus on one or two specific approaches as a maximum.
   b. we examine every aspect of personality from a biological perspective.
   c. we focus our attention on the cognitive approach.
   d. we examine personality from several different perspectives.

2. Some of Freud's concepts are relevant and interesting when

   a. viewed in terms of genetic predispositions.
   b. viewed in terms of cognitive psychology.
   c. viewed as a set of ego defense mechanisms.
   d. none of the above

3. A necessary part of the cognitive explanation for the transference phenomenon is

   a. a strong cognitive representation of people.
   b. the activation of self-schemas.
   c. the repression of traumatic events deep in the unconscious.
   d. the failure to reach self-actualization.

4. Which of the following statements is true about transference?

   a. People transfer negative emotions to strangers who resemble unknown persons.
   b. Transference takes place without our awareness.
   c. Transference can alter the way we behave around others.
   d. all of the above

5. Billy is a repressor and is required by his sixth-grade teacher to give a three-minute speech about the worst aspect of his own personality. According to research, how anxious will Billy get over this speech assignment?

   a. His self-report scores on emotion scales will show a great degree of anxiety.
   b. His blood pressure will show calm compared to nonrepressors.
   c. It depends on how his anxiety response is measured.
   d. It is impossible to tell.

6. Although repressors characteristically have a strong reaction to thoughts that are not pleasant, they

   a. cannot push these thoughts out of awareness.
   b. typically respond with more emotion than is appropriate.
   c. somehow succeed in pushing these thoughts out of awareness.
   d. both b and c

7. According to gender schema theory, people are likely to perceive, evaluate, and organize information as sex-typed if

   a. they are highly masculine.
   b. they are highly feminine.
   c. they are both highly masculine and highly feminine.
   d. either a or b

8. Because sex-typed and non-sex-typed people differ in the strength of their gender schemas, we should expect that

    a. sex-typed people describe behaviors as either masculine or feminine.
    b. non-sex-typed people recall gender-related information better.
    c. sex-typed people are less likely to notice inconsistencies in gender-related behavior.
    d. all of the above

9. In research on clustering and gender schemas, which of the following types of people were more likely to cluster words on a list according to gender?

    a. sex-typed
    b. cross-sex-typed
    c. androgynous
    d. undifferentiated

10. Research on recall for events between men and women has shown that men have better recall of __________ than women.

    a. personal events
    b. sporting events
    c. impersonal events
    d. emotional events

11. Which of the following is *false* about emotional memories?

    a. Women attend to and process information about emotions more than men.
    b. The links between emotional memories are stronger for men than women.
    c. Both happy and sad memories are more accessible for women than men.
    d. Recalling one sad experience is more likely to trigger another sad memory for women than for men.

12. When researchers gave participants a camera and asked them to take photographs that described themselves,

    a. women's photos were more likely to include activities than men's.
    b. women's photos were more likely to include other people than men's.
    c. men's photos were more likely to include objects rather than themselves.
    d. none of the above

13. According to the cognitive approach to depression, processing information through the depressive schema

    a. causes people to become depressed.
    b. causes people to generate even more depressing thoughts.
    c. leads people to ignore positive information.
    d. all of the above

14. In research investigating the recall of words in depressed people, which was *not* a group that recalled depression-related words better than normals?

    a. clinically depressed patients
    b. mildly depressed college students
    c. nondepressed patients
    d. students simply asked to think about some sad events

15. George is feeling very depressed as he drives home from work very tired. As he approaches an intersection in traffic, he can see flashing red lights ahead although the reason for the lights is not immediately apparent. How will George likely interpret this ambiguous information?

    a. with negative and pessimistic thoughts
    b. with curiosity
    c. with positive ideas about getting home another way
    d. with disinterest in the possibility someone could be injured

16. The simple model used to explain animal learned helplessness was inadequate for learned helplessness in humans because

    a. humans always respond to uncontrollable situations with learned helplessness.
    b. feelings of learned helplessness generalize to some tasks but not others.
    c. conditioning often leads to learned helplessness in humans.
    d. cognitive models of learned helplessness cannot be applied to animals.

17. Which of the following attributions tends to lead to learned helplessness?

    a. internal attributions
    b. unstable attributions
    c. specific attributions
    d. none of the above

18. Which of the following is an external, stable attribution for a student's failure on their midterm exam?

    a. The professor made the test too hard.
    b. I do not like this course anyway.
    c. I'm not smart enough to understand the material.
    d. The students who performed well were lucky.

19. Pessimists tend to have which explanatory style?

    a. external, stable, and specific
    b. external, stable, and global
    c. internal, stable, and global
    d. internal, unstable, and global

20. In a study of college students' reactions to their midterm grades, researchers found
   a. only depressed students showed an increase in depressed mood immediately after getting negative feedback.
   b. nondepressed students with a specific explanatory style became depressed and remained so after two days.
   c. students in general showed an increase in depressed mood immediately after getting negative feedback.
   d. depressed students modified their explanatory style to be more specific.

Integrative Questions

1. If you sought treatment from a humanistic psychotherapist, how would your therapist explain transference and how would that explanation be different from that given by a cognitive therapist? (472-474)

2. Discuss the basic ideas behind gender schema theory. What features of this theory make it clearly a cognitive theory? That is, how are cognitive personality theorists' ideas incorporated into gender schema theory? (480-482)

3. What are some of the continuing issues in the area of gender schema theory? Discuss the merits of some alternatives to the standard theory. Specify how the Rep test is used to assess gender schemas. (480-482)

4. How does the depressive schema work? Contrast the outlook on life between most normal people and depressed individuals. Make a list of all the many predictions of depressive schema theory. (488-491)

5. Explain the attributional model of learned helplessness depression by contrasting the several attributions that are possible. How does explanatory style play a role in learned helplessness and what is its relationship to pessimism? (491-495)

Evaluative Questions

1. If we assume that the cognitive explanation for repression is accurate, what does that tell us about Freud's original conception? In other words, discuss the implications for Freudian theory's cornerstone if cognitive theory is correct. (475-479)

2. Summarize and critically evaluate the several results of research on differences in gender schemas. List the various methods and consider alternative explanations for each result. Do you think you are sex-typed? Why or why not? (480-482)

3. State whether depressed people process information through a specific depressive schema or simply through negative schemas in general. Give evidence from research to support your answer. What is the evidence from research on the accessibility of depressing memories? (482-484, 487-491)

4. Consider a situation in your recent past in which you failed to accomplish some task. From Table 16.1 on page 493 of the text, identify the kind of attribution you made about your failure. What implications does your attribution have in terms of your own explanatory style? (492-494)

Answers to Multiple Choice Questions

1. d, 471
2. b, 472
3. a, 473
4. d, 474
5. c, 475
6. c, 476
7. d, 480
8. a, 480
9. a, 481
10. c, 482
11. b, 483
12. b, 486
13. d, 488
14. c, 489
15. a, 491
16. b, 492
17. a, 492
18. d, 493
19. c, 494
20. c, 494

Chapter 17

Some Concluding Observations

Personality Theories as Tools

Personality Theory

Personality Research

Conclusion

Learning Objectives

1. Discuss the use of personality theory as an explanatory tool in everyday behavior. Explain why psychologists rarely find one agreed-upon answer to questions of why people act the way they do.
2. Define what is meant by an "eclectic" approach in psychotherapy. State the reason many therapists identify themselves as eclectic.
3. State the general trends and current status of each of the major theoretical approaches to personality. Specify which continue in popularity and which are in decline. Indicate which of these approaches seem to be blending together and why this may be so.
4. Present three signs of growing consensus among personality researchers. Include in your discussion the general feeling in the field about the person and the situation and the status of thoughts outside of awareness.
5. Summarize the more recent research and theory on achievement from various approaches to personality.
6. Summarize the more recent research and theory on social relationships from various approaches to personality. State what each approach predicts about human relationships.

7. Summarize the more recent research and theory on the psychology of well-being from various approaches to personality. List and briefly discuss each of the major predicting factors.
8. Summarize the more recent research on behaviors related to one's physical health. Briefly explain how negative affect, locus of control, and self-disclosure are related to health problems according to research.

Important Concepts

eclectic (p. 498)
"trait" debate (p. 499)
third force (p. 500)
blank slate (p. 500)
"social cognitive" theory (p. 500)
"person-situation" debate (p. 501)

InfoTrac *Search terms:*

psychotherapy (p. 499)
interpersonal attraction (p. 503)

Programmed Review

Although each perspective on personality provides relevant information for describing human personality, no one perspective can give a _________ picture.

complete — p. 498

The number of traits identified by researchers and the tests developed to measure these traits _________.

continue to grow — p. 499

The original declaration of the humanistic psychologists that their _________ would rival and eventually replace the psychoanalytic and behavioral approaches has not come true.

third force — p. 500

Today personality researchers have made a persuasive case that _________ cannot be easily ignored.

genetic influences — p. 501

Psychoanalytic, humanistic, and cognitive therapists generally work to help clients _________ their troubling thoughts.

bring to awareness — p. 502

Many researchers have examined _________ by looking at how people react to failure.

achievement behavior p. 503

People who suffer from _________ want more social contact but often lack the skills necessary to establish satisfying relationships.

loneliness p. 504

Recent work on attachment styles suggests that our childhood experiences with caregivers can determine our ways at looking at _________ .

adult relationships p. 504

One component of Type A that is a relatively strong predictor of health problems is _________.

anger and hostility p. 505

The personality psychologist's old axiom is: "There are few differences between people, but what differences there are __________ ."

really matter p. 506

Multiple Choice Questions

1. The question for students of personality is not "Which theory is correct?" but rather
   a. "Which theory makes the most sense to me?"
   b. "How do the theories combine to explain any given behavior?"
   c. "How can each approach to personality help me better understand behavior?"
   d. "Why do some perspectives fail to give the answers?"

2. One fact that points to the continued importance of the psychoanalytic approach is that
   a. neo-Freudian theories have not been able to replace it.
   b. the use of projective tests is still popular among therapists.
   c. the cognitive approach to personality has not achieved general acceptance.
   d. the only alternatives are the behavioral and humanistic approaches.

3. Which approach has assisted the development of the Big Five Model of personality structure?

   a. psychoanalytic
   b. behavioral
   c. cognitive
   d. trait

4. _________ increasingly acknowledge the importance of concepts they once rejected.

   a. Psychoanalysts
   b. Behaviorists
   c. Humanistic therapists
   d. Social learning theorists

5. Today social learning theory is at times difficult to distinguish from

   a. humanistic psychology.
   b. the biological approach.
   c. the trait approach.
   d. the cognitive approach.

6. The current popularity of the _________ approach is a general trend that is reflected in courses in developmental, social, and abnormal psychology.

   a. cognitive
   b. biological
   c. social learning
   d. trait

7. One of the general ideas about the nature of human personality that is gaining acceptance among theorists from all perspectives is

   a. the importance of thoughts outside of awareness.
   b. the genetic influences on personality.
   c. the interaction between the person and the situation.
   d. all of the above

8. Which of the following best describes the current status of the person-situation debate?

   a. The person contributes more to behavior because of the growing recognition of genetic influences.
   b. The situation contributes more to behavior because of the growing understanding of conditioning processes.
   c. The situation is less important for domain-specific features of personality.
   d. An interaction of person and situation determines behavior.

9. People with defensive pessimism

    a. are less likely to give up in the face of a negative evaluation.
    b. generally do better on achievement tests than optimists.
    c. do best when allowed to think about all that might go wrong.
    d. are driven to master achievement tasks.

10. In Western cultures, how satisfied people are with their lives tends to be a function of

    a. childhood experiences.
    b. genetic influences.
    c. self-esteem.
    d. personal constructs.

11. Recent research on gender type shows which of the following make the best romantic partners?

    a. feminine
    b. feminine and androgynous
    c. masculine and androgynous
    d. masculine

12. Studies of ___________ indicate that internals and externals typically have different ideas about their role in maintaining physical health.

    a. attributional style
    b. self-schemas
    c. extraversion
    d. locus of control

Integrative Questions

1. Discuss three general ideas acknowledged by theorists from different perspectives that represent a growing consensus in personality research and theory. (501-502)

2. Indicate how different approaches to researching personality integrate to give us a better understanding of behaviors related to achievement and relationships. (503)

3. Indicate the integration of different approaches to personality to give us a better understanding of behaviors related to well-being and physical health. (504-506)

Evaluative Questions

1. Think of an everyday question you have about people and their behavior (i.e., like the question in the text: Why do people keep pets?). Use personality theory as a tool to understand the answer to your question. List six theoretical perspectives and state what theorists within each approach would say today about the behavior of people in your question. (498-501)

2. Summarize the current status of each of the major theoretical approaches to personality. With which do you most agree? Support your answer. (499-502)

3. Speculate about the future of personality research and theory. Given what you know about current trends in psychology and the rapid changes in our society, what do you think the future picture is like? Is it possible that some of the established perspectives will merge? If so, in what ways do you think they will come together? (502-506)

Answers to Multiple Choice Questions

1. c, 498
2. b, 499
3. d, 499
4. b, 500
5. d, 500
6. a, 500
7. d, 501
8. d, 501
9. c, 503
10. c, 505
11. b, 504
12. d, 506

InfoTrac Flowchart

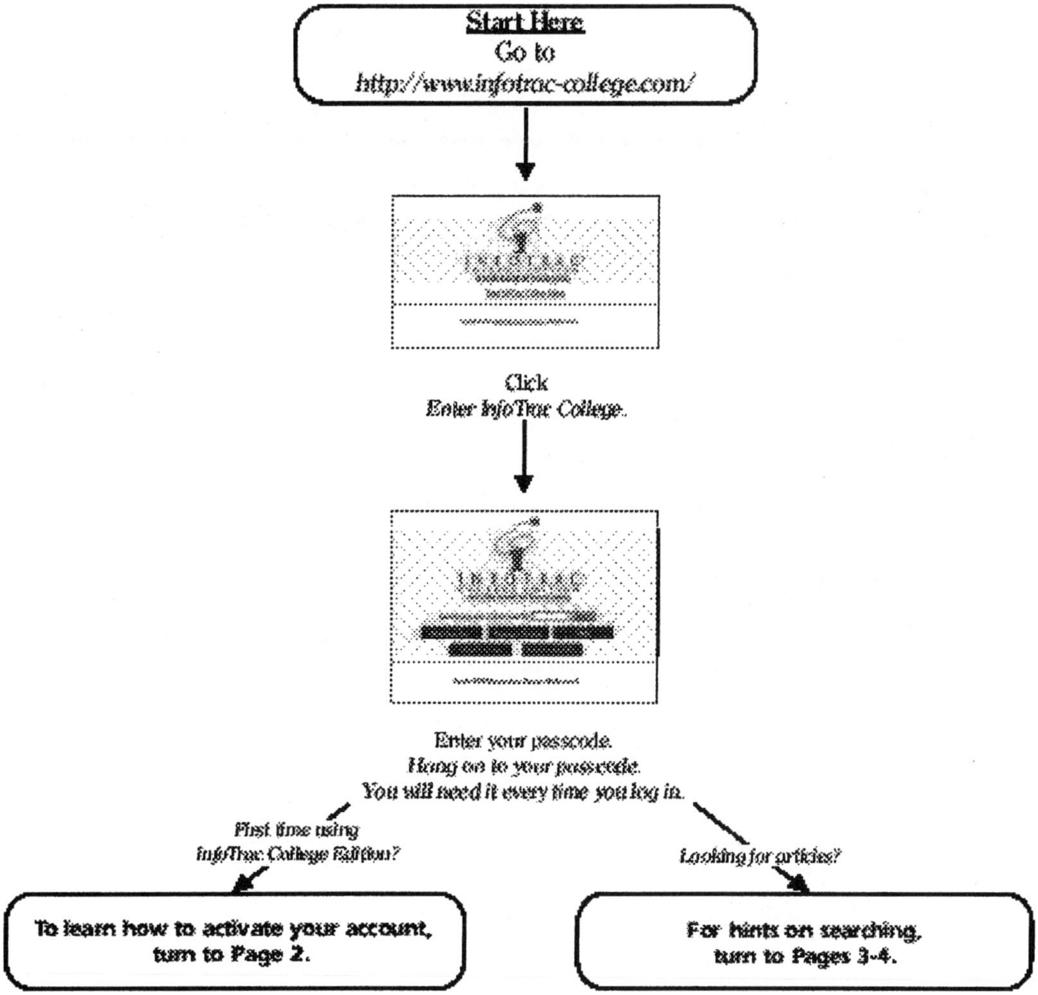